# RELATIVIST AND ABSOLUTIST

EMERSON R. MARKS

# RELATIVIST &
# ABSOLUTIST

## THE EARLY NEOCLASSICAL
## DEBATE IN ENGLAND

RUTGERS UNIVERSITY PRESS

*New Brunswick, New Jersey* - - - *1955*

*To*
MARY

# Foreword

Whatever else may ultimately be said of it, the literary criticism of this generation has been vital. And as in other periods when discussion of literature has flourished, questions involving the principles underlying the discussion have been raised. Inevitably, whenever debate about poetry has been sufficiently widespread and protracted, the participants have felt the need to formulate some kind of poetic—if only to meet the challenge of their opponents. Expositions of dramatic structure, evaluations of novels, explications of poems, themselves suggest to those who undertake them (or to others) the explicit statement of an aesthetic in terms of which the expositions may be understood, the evaluations justified, the explications made significant.

Intensive criticism of literature, in other words, leads sooner or later to what has been called criticism of criticism. Arguments about the nature or value of literary works are often seen to arise from more fundamental differences of critical method or doctrine. The melee of individual critics thus tends to evolve into the more orderly, if equally inconclusive, debate among "schools," in which the issues are those of basic aesthetic theory. In recent years, one such issue has been receiving more conscious and exclusive attention than ever before. Among his strictures on Cleanth Brooks' theory of paradox, Herbert J. Muller objects to its absolutism,[1] thus posing a critical question that has long been traditional though not always so directly and abstractly discussed.

The fight between relativist and absolutist has not been an equal one. In general, English criticism, after the tentative groping for standards described by G. Gregory Smith in his introduction to *Elizabethan Critical Essays*, becomes and long remains predominantly absolutist. Until the later seventeenth century at least, critics typically assumed that there was one method of writing, for instance, a good tragedy: one method that always had been and always would be correct, one that could be departed from only in unessentials. And a single way in creation implied a single and universal set of criteria in appraisal. Only part of the whisper of dissent from this view that becomes a chorus by the middle of the next century is on relativist grounds; and of those critics who do advance relativist arguments in the earlier neoclassical period, few seem to have been aware of their theoretical implications. Such awareness is a gradual achievement. In his *Idiom of Poetry* (1941), a work of critical relativism, Professor Frederick Pottle calls attention to the comparative modernity of his approach as a consciously and consistently held critical method. It is fully exemplified, he declares, by no major English critic, though Dryden *might* have adopted such a method had he realized the promise of his earliest criticism. But just as the intellectual climate was against Dryden's relativist tendencies, so Professor Pottle finds in twentieth century scientific relativity a compelling argument for abandoning absolutist aesthetics in our day.

Although Professor Pottle declares his adherence to absolutism in matters of faith and morals, one might add that the increasing suspicion of absolute values in those areas during the nineteenth and twentieth centuries has undoubtedly helped to place the avowedly absolutist critic frequently on the defensive. But even if, as he seems to imply, Pottle's book is the first deliberate attempt in English to apply one kind of critical relativism systematically to a branch of literature, relativist arguments appear in English criticism as early as the seventeenth century, and, in isolated instances, even earlier. In the ensuing chapters I have tried to investigate their origins, to distinguish their kinds, and to relate them to several contemporary cultural forces during a period from the late sixteenth to the early eighteenth centuries.

I do not intend a defense of relativist criticism. On the contrary, the drift of ideas in this early stage indicates not only that it was, but that it is likely to remain, a minor theme. Professor Pottle's failure to discover a consistent relativist among the great English critics is probably more significant than his remarks indicate. In critical practice relativism is frequent, if not consistent. But the essential denial of universality implied in the term would seem to clash with the very thing any theory aims at: the postulation of a law valid for every instance included in a type. There need be no conscious recourse to any absolutism when the critic is asking how this particular poem functions or what is valuable in it. But the question why it deserves to be called a poem at all, what qualities it shares with thousands of other poems, leads finally to an attempt at a definition of a type—some absolute statement. And this question has sooner or later always been asked.

But if the relativist faces this obstacle, the absolutist has suffered from other embarrassments. There have been, for example, many absolutist theories, a fact which in itself challenges absolutism. The resulting dilemma has led Professors René Wellek and Austin Warren, who reject Pottle's thesis, to suggest the *tertium quid* of "perspectivism," which sees a literary work in reference to the values of its own and of subsequent ages, sees it as dynamic, "full of possibilities." [2]

# Foreword

Viewed historically, each dominant absolutist theory appears to have faced a relativist attack of mounting intensity which ended not in the establishment of relativism but in the substitution of a new absolutism, designed, among other things, to meet the relativist objections. The process is thus roughly cyclical. I have sought to deal with the first of these broad cycles in modern English criticism.

So much for the occasion of this book. It may be well to add a few words about its purpose and method. It was undertaken in the belief that a historical and analytical study of the earliest manifestations of relativist criticism (apart from its intrinsic interest) might help to clarify the current discussion. The breadth and intricacy of the subject precluded both exhaustive treatment of the material and any pretense of settling the question. The conclusions are offered more in the hope of isolating and elucidating the data relevant to the problem than as a final solution. The procedure is perhaps best explained by a secondary purpose. The history of criticism, it seems to me, might profitably be written from the point of view of recurring issues rather than in terms of the peculiar characteristics of the critical writing of successive periods. The present study is an essay (in the older sense) at doing this for one chapter of that history, and it is limited, moreover, to one issue.

Since its completion, I have come upon a passage which puts this better, and certainly with more authority, than I can do. "We can examine the critical writings of the past," R. S. Crane observes, "not merely doctrinally and circumstantially but methodologically as well—i.e., as successive efforts to cope with perennial problems of the literary arts and their products by means of principles of formulation and proof which, however they may differ from critic to critic or period to period, can yet be stated and compared in universal terms independently of the

shifting particulars of the discourses in which they function. And a history of criticism of this sort . . . can be
made to serve a number of important purposes in the education of critics beyond the mere satisfaction of their historical curiosity." [3]

This is a large order, far from filled in the following
pages. But perhaps they suggest that the critics of an earlier
time dealt significantly with at least one of the "perennial
problems of the literary arts."

EMERSON R. MARKS

Nutley, New Jersey
Spring, 1955

# Acknowledgments

I wish to record several kinds of indebtedness. Some of it, especially that to teachers, is perhaps no longer quite consciously felt and thus impossible to assess. But, in attempting a study which touches upon important aspects of seventeenth century thought, I owe much to the richly informed and provocative teaching of Professor Walter MacKellar of New York University. And to those who know something of literary theory it will suffice to say that I entered the graduate school of the University of Iowa in 1941 to find Professors Norman Foerster, Austin Warren, and René Wellek on its staff. Two of these, Professors Warren and Wellek, read the manuscript. For their kind encouragement and advice I am especially grateful. Thanks are due also to Professor Gellert S. Alleman, friend and Rutgers colleague, for his unfailing patience during the many months I made free with his expert knowledge of bibliographical technique and his fine private library. To the book's faults of matter and manner I must, of course, lay exclusive claim.

I wish finally to express my appreciation to the Rutgers Research Council, which provided a generous grant toward publication.

E. R. M.

# Contents

*Foreword*                                             vii

1  Critical Relativism and Historical Criticism        3

2  Elizabethan Rudiments                                8

3  Ends and Means                                      26

4  Relativism of Ends                                  50

5  The Sources of Early Relativism                     70

6  The Idea of Progress                                92

7  The New Absolutism                                 115

8  Conclusion                                         127

*Notes*                                               131

*List of Works Cited*                                 157

*Index*                                               165

RELATIVIST AND ABSOLUTIST

# Chapter 1

# Critical Relativism and

# Historical Criticism

Two terms have been commonly and improperly equated. Not all historical criticism is relativist, nor is all relativist criticism historical. Historical consciousness in criticism, spasmodic and infrequent before 1600, was well developed and widespread by the middle of the eighteenth century. Literature, it was felt, partook of development, or even, like science, of progress. When this notion is used as an argument against applying to the literature of one age the critical criteria established in another, the result may be a plea for relativism. But it may also lead simply to the substitution of a new absolutism in place of the old. The history of criticism is replete with instances of the historical point of view in absolutist theory and practice, notably in recent times.

One line of thought supporting this confusion of concepts [1] runs thus: the notion of progress stimulated the study of history, including in due course the history of literature; the resulting historical sense, seeing all human institutions not static but mutable, was, and remains, incompatible with absolute criteria of value. Whatever logic this argument may possess, it was not always followed. Many critics writing in the triumphant early days of the new science, hearty believers in the doctrine of progress and its application to literature, were uncompromisingly absolutist. Roughly, they fall into two groups: those who attributed poetry's failure to equal the progress of the sciences to the poet's refusal to abide by the Rules; [2] and those who believed in an advance to a final perfection not dreamed of by the Ancients. Neither group admits the notion of a varying measure. For the second group, for instance, Sophocles' tragedies would be inferior in the light of the final perfect "idea" toward which tragedy would progress.

A second source of misunderstanding can perhaps be traced to confused thinking about the critical function itself. The boundaries of the critic's province are notoriously vague. Despite many attempts to restrict his office, he has in practice performed a plural task. Criticism is obviously evaluation. But it is also analysis, and though these two functions are necessarily joined in most good criticism, analysis does exist alone. When a critic applies his knowledge of history to *explaining* his author's work, when he sees it to some extent a resultant of contemporary conditions, he is not, so far, applying a relativist aesthetic. He may, in fact, join to such "historical" analysis a judgment by absolute standards.[3] Dryden and Dennis, to name only two, explained many things in Shakespeare by reference to his times. But this was by way of accounting for "faults." The reader was not invited to

4

make an appropriate adjustment of the scale, to read into his measure of the older dramatist's achievement a historical "correction"; he was at best urged to tolerate a great master's violations of an aesthetic universally valid.

Moreover, even when a critic became convinced that the cultural climate peculiar to a given period made the reigning aesthetic irrelevant to the appraisal of its literature, he did not always resort to relativism. He concluded rather that the received theories were invalid not only for the period in question but for any period, and sought forthwith to formulate new ones equally absolute but presumably truer. A case in point is Dryden's remark that Aristotle might have changed his mind about his pity-and-terror theory of tragedy "if he had seen ours." The "Heads of an Answer to Rymer" (where this appears) contains relativism, but this is not an instance of it. Part of Dryden's objection to Rymer's application of ancient standards to modern drama is that they are no longer relevant; but some of it is that they are not entirely *correct*. "He therefore unjustly blames us for not building on what the ancients left us; for it seems, upon consideration of the premises, that we have wholly finished what they began." [4]

Simply put, the distinction lies in this dual nature of the critical act. And we may generalize by saying that when certain peculiarities of a writer's temporal and local environment are considered in *passing judgment* on his work, we have relativist criticism. When they are applied only to elucidation, analysis, or explanation, we have historical but not relativist criticism. The latter term has proper reference only to the specific act of evaluation.

Further justification for insisting on this distinction of definitions can be found in the varying histories of the two types. Historical criticism, in the sense used here, has had a full and complex development, intimately bound up with that of literary history.[5] For perhaps two centuries critics have studied problems like the genesis of theme, genre, and style in terms of historical conditions. They have gone, that is, to history—the history of institutions and the history of ideas—to account for literary phenomena by a method analogous to the scientific. By contrast, the history of relativist literary criticism would yield a thin volume. Professor Frederick Pottle could declare, as late as 1946, that "none of the great English critics can be held in all respects to exemplify" critical relativism.[6]

In addition to the difference of sheer bulk between these two kinds, there is a difference in development. Criticism as a whole is concerned with both theory and practice. The historical approach was applied to specific works as early as it was defended as a generally valuable method, if not earlier. Relativism, on the other hand, is represented largely by theoretical pronouncements, with examples of its application few and unelaborated. Writers are not lacking who urge the use of varying criteria, but, perhaps because of the difficulty and subtlety of the process, they seldom make the experiment. And when they do, the result in most cases is a criticism defensive and negative. That is, the rela-

6

tivist idea is used as an argument to suspend judgment (usually unfavorable) of an author rather than to demonstrate positive values in his work overlooked or misinterpreted by the absolutist. Examination of the actual critical literature of the last three hundred years, then, suggests distinguishing between relativist and nonrelativist historical criticism because of a marked difference in the amount of each produced and in the frequency with which theory is reduced to practice.

Finally, though here the line is often hard to draw, there is a certain amount of nonhistorical relativism. Such is the approach attacked by some scholars as "mere" impressionism, the theory of individual taste. Thomas Hobbes, for one, believed that beauty was entirely subjective, and therefore relative to the temperament of the individual. Subjective relativism of this kind is infrequent in neoclassical times. Since it ultimately makes any objective standards impossible, it does not become an important element in critical practice until the post-Romantic vogue of aesthetic lawlessness. Its prevalence during the late nineteenth century, in the form of "adventures of one's soul among masterpieces," is well known.

# Chapter 2

# Elizabethan Rudiments

At this late date there is no need to labor the disparity between Elizabethan literary production and Elizabethan literary theory. It is enough to recall that an age of creative maturity and consummation was also an age of critical adolescence. But if, with a few notable exceptions, sixteenth century Englishmen failed to provide answers of lasting cogency to the fundamental critical questions, they did at least raise most of the questions. Their attempts to elaborate largely failed; but, perhaps because they were groping, they touched upon many things.

Unlike their counterparts in later periods, the Elizabethan critics could make few if any general assumptions.[1] The growing acquaintance with the classical literature and languages served in many cases to induce a feeling of inferiority about the native product. Awe of the mighty pagans tended to contempt for past English literature and indifference to contemporary work. The Puritan attack was not alone in placing poetry's friends on the defensive. It was even debatable whether the native literature was worthy of serious consideration.

As late as 1589 George Puttenham felt impelled to devote a chapter of his *Arte* to convincing his readers that

8

"there may be an art of our English Poesie, aswell as there is of the Latine and Greeke." For to construct an "art," to impose on the growing modern poetry an order comparable to that of the ancient, remained throughout the century a prime concern. In such a situation, as the evidence abundantly shows, the temptation to adopt the entire classical aesthetic was strong. But it was not unresisted. "The saving quality of this incipient classicism," Gregory Smith writes, ". . . is that it is not extreme. . . . They have a genuine conviction of their inefficiency, and though they play with dogma, which in the immediate future became the creed of a militant criticism, they seldom forget that they cannot claim to be more than experimenters." Besides this diffidence, there was at least a suspicion that the classical dogmas might not always apply to modern work. Smith notes: "The unwillingness to have rigid rules, whether in the choice of subject, in language, or in prosody. . . . The caution against interference with existing habit, against drawing Poetry by the ears, is not only Sidney's and Daniel's, but the commonplace of this collection of essays." [2]

There was nonetheless little question that some kind of order was needed; and order meant rules, rules for writing and rules for judging. While the strong national pride of the period generated a desire to emulate the best, the dominant humanism of the earlier part of Elizabeth's reign could accept only the Greek and Latin masterpieces as worthy models of excellence. Thus for Roger Ascham, in 1570, mediaeval romances were vain and immoral; rhyme, because it was eschewed by the matchless

Ancients, "Gothic" and barbarous. Since there was no question of surpassing these giants, excellence could be achieved only by imitating them. Indeed, says Ascham, Virgil himself, by rejecting Ennius and following the Greeks, had done that very thing and thereby added glory to the Roman name.[3]

The Humanists' interest in style and versification was fundamentally moral, not aesthetic. Rhetoric was important because it was intimately bound up with ethic. The history of Greek and Latin shows that "whan apte and good wordes began to be neglected . . . than also began ill deedes to spring, strange maners to oppresse good orders, newe and fond opinions to striue with olde and trewe doctrine, first in Philosophie and after in Religion, right iudgment of all thinges to be peruerted. . . ."[4] This provides another key to Ascham's essential position. Truth is one, not many. So therefore is the manner of its expression.

But between *The Scholemaster* and the end of the century much had occurred to challenge the logic of this absolutism.[5] Many critics were aware that England had in the meantime produced a body of fine lyric and dramatic poetry which it was difficult or impossible to square with ancient precept. This might have led to a scaling down of the ancient poets and a correction or rejection of Aristotelian-Horatian poetics, as it did later. But the time to sit in judgment on the demigods of the past or question the ipse dixit was not yet. The result was a primitive kind of relativism: there must be, they concluded, a "variety of ways."

Ascham's scornful dismissal of rhyme was hardly more effective in forestalling debate than it was in preventing the practice. The rhyme-blank verse question was part of the larger question of prosody, itself an aspect of the still larger one of the relationship of language to the poetic art. It is possible to trace a tenuous but persistent thread of what might be called a prosodic or even a linguistic relativism through the critical writing of this period. Like much of the relativism before 1600, it is largely a protest, a reaction against something much more dominant. The humanist conviction that modern literature could be valuable only as it resembled the ancient logically enough included what Saintsbury has called "The Craze for Classical Metres." [6]

Gabriel Harvey, in his fourth "Familiar Letter," protests the violence done to established usage by accenting English words according to Latin rules.[7] Thus even in the work of one of the reformers is an insistence that a quantitative prosody must recognize that English is not Latin. But Harvey, himself a victim of the "craze," does not follow out the logic of his position: that the prosodic value of any poetry is relative to its linguistic medium. Richard Stanyhurst, who had to face the matter squarely in translating Virgil, comes somewhat closer to a general relativist view. In his dedication he anticipates criticism from "Precisians," and in his preface "To thee Learned Reader" he writes: "Wherefor syth thee *poëtes* theymselves advouch . . . that *Art* is . . . bound too shape yt self by al imitation too *Nature,* wee must request theese *grammatical Precisians,* that as euery countrye hath his

11

peculiar law, so they permit euerye language too vse his particular loare." "Peculiar" is a key word in the relativist dialectic. The fact of peculiarity and particularity denies universal and absolute authority to any standard. But, though his statement contains a *point de repère* of every relativist, Stanyhurst is hardly more relativist than Harvey. To maintain otherwise is to overlook his avowal that in translating Virgil he is taking Ascham's advice to beautify "oure English language with heroical verses." The possible implications of his generalization about "peculiar law" and "particular loare" escape him; he offers it only to justify his refusal to be as "stieflie tyed too thee ordinaunces of thee Latins" as the strictest classicists might wish.[8]

William Webbe continues the campaign for a classical prosody in his *Discourse of English Poetrie* (1586). Classicist and absolute, he knows and approves of Harvey's attempt at reform. Nonetheless, he admits rhyme because, "beeing so ingraffed by custome, and frequented by the most parte, I may not vtterly dissalowe it, least I should seeme to call in question the iudgement of all our famous wryters, which haue wonne eternall prayse by theyr memorable workes compyled in that verse." This passage illustrates perfectly the embarrassment felt by those committed to a simple one-to-one ratio between Latin and Greek practice and poetic theory in general. The theory makes no provision for rhyme, and Webbe is personally convinced that its use has been a serious deterrent to attaining "that good order of versifying."[9] Yet, unaccountably, readers delight in it and good writers affect it; it works.

Had English poets applied themselves, Webbe argues, the English might by his day have evolved "the true kind of versifying in immitation of the Greekes and Latines." He is aware of the objection that English words do not lend themselves to the formation of classical feet, but replies that the ancient rules may be altered to suit. The main thing is to construct a foot-quantity verse as like the classical as possible. Besides, he concludes, careful examination shows that English words *are* quite suitable to the principal Latin and Greek metres.[10] Throughout the whole *Discourse* there is no hint that its author ever entertained the thought that poetic structure was a function of such historical forces as the native literary tradition or the nature of the language; still less that these forces should influence appraisal or suggest the local irrelevancy of the ancient system. He appends the Horatian "Cannons" to his essay with full faith in their universal validity.

George Puttenham's *The Arte of English Poesie* (1589) is characteristic of the criticism of its time in many respects. One of these is an inconsistency [11] of theoretical position which permits calling him relativist only with reservations. He does possess enough historical sense to see, however crudely, some relationship between literary production and contemporary nonliterary factors, as when he complains that poetry languishes in his day for lack of the princely favor it enjoyed in the past. With much more conviction than his predecessors, he argues that prosodic form is a function of linguistic peculiarities. The Greeks' quantitative versification arose from their predominantly polysyllabic language, whereas, owing to the frequency of "Saxon" monosyllables in English, "there could be no such obseruation of times in the sound of our wordes, & for that cause we could not haue the feete which the Greeks and Latines haue in their meetres." [12] More positively, he declares that this very monosyllabic nature of English lends itself to rhyme, a modern compensation for the loss of Greek *"rithme* or numerositie." [13]

This is prosodic relativism, for it postulates the practical inapplicability of the classical prosodic techniques to modern English verse. It is relativist, and not merely historical, criticism because it entails consequences for evaluation. The sound and movement of a poem being one source of its value, its prosody is a pertinent element in appraising it. When Puttenham argues, in effect, that the aesthetic value inherent in prosody as such is produced in different ways in a Latin and an English poem, he is denying us the right to condemn the one by the rules of the other, as Ascham had done. He is, in sum, taking a relativist position with respect to at least one source of poetic value.

And yet, not always. Paradoxically enough, the *Arte* contains an absolutist argument for rhyme as well. Like the more celebrated essay of Samuel Daniel, Puttenham's work is designed primarily to defend the dignity and promote the good estate of his country's literature. Not centrally concerned with critical theory, he is untroubled, provided he can further his purpose, by theoretical in-

14

congruities. Early in his book he defends rhyme by brief arguments from antiquity and from "nature."

> And the Greeke and Latine Poesie was by verse numerous and metricall, running vpon pleasant feete, sometimes swift, sometime slow (their words very aptly seruing that purpose) but without any rime or tunable concord in th'end of their verses, as we and all other nations now vse. But the Hebrues & Chaldees, who were more ancient then the Greekes, did not only vse a metricall Poesie, but also with the same a maner of rime, as hath bene of late obserued by learned men. Whereby it appeareth that our vulgar running Poesie was common to all the nations of the world besides, whom the Latines and Greekes in speciall called barbarous. So as it was, notwithstanding, the first and most ancient Poesie, and the most vniuersall; which two points do otherwise giue to all humane inuentions and affaires no small credit.

The use of rhyme among primitive peoples, he adds,

> proues also that our maner of vulgar Poesie is more ancient then the artificiall of the Greeks and Latines, ours comming by instinct of nature, which was before Art or obseruation, and vsed with the sauage and vnciuill, who were before all science or ciuilitie. . . .[14]

Avowedly, Puttenham's point is only to establish that the modern prosody "is no lesse to be allowed and commended then theirs," i.e., the classical. But his appeals to antiquity, to nature, and to universality (then almost impregnable arguments for "truth") would in effect demonstrate the absolute superiority of the modern way.

Still, he is not concerned deliberately to do anything of the kind. Puttenham wishes only to prove that the native tradition in versification ought not to be scorned, that it is as "respectable" and as well adapted to its language as the ancient. The absolutist note would appear to be injected as a matter of clever rhetoric: the hint that rhyme is better may at least win hostile readers to concede that it is as good.

However much Puttenham felt obliged to hedge on the question, for some Elizabethans there was no doubt that the rules of classical versification possessed no absolute status. Thomas Nash's pithy reply to Harvey, in *Foure Letters Confuted* (1592), is typical of their reasoning: "The Hexamiter verse I graunt to be a Gentleman of an auncient house (so is many an english begger); yet this Clyme of ours hee cannot thriue in. Our speech is too craggy for him to set his plough in; hee goes twitching and hopping in our language like a man running vpon quagmiers . . . retaining no part of that stately smooth gate which he vaunts himselfe with amongst the Greeks and Latins." The hexametre of Homer and Virgil, he therefore concludes, is no touchstone for censuring the verse of Chaucer and Spenser.[15]

Thomas Campion's *Observations in the Art of English Poesie* (1602) has been justly named the "most interesting result of the 'new versifying' craze,"[16] because it draws the theoretical lines of debate more clearly than ever before. The controversy, presumably, was now old enough for Campion to see the essential issue. He is clearly and logically absolutist, not blindly so. He appreciates and concedes the arguments from established usage and from the nature of the language. In fact, he insists on the latter. The failure of the experiments with the dactyl in

English, he writes, is "no wonder, seeing it is an attempt altogether against the nature of our language. For both the concurse of our monasillables make our verses vnapt to slide, and also, if we examine our polysillables, we shall finde few of them, by reason of their heauinesse, willing to serue in place of a *Dactile*." [17]

But difficulties of this kind are minor matters for Campion, as is the argument from "the consent of many nations." "All this and more can not yet deterre me from a lawful defence of *perfection,* or make me any whit the sooner adheare to that which is lame and vnbeseeming. For custome I alleage that ill vses are to be abolisht, and that *things naturally imperfect* can not be perfected by vse. Old customes, *if they be better,* why should they not be recald, as the yet florishing custome of numerous poesy vsed among the *Romanes* and *Grecians?*" [18] The phrases here italicized (except the proper names) reveal the fundamental absolutism of Campion's reasoning. For him, no objections could weigh against the adoption of what was per se "perfect," "better"; by the same token, no incidental advantages could justify retaining "things naturally imperfect."

By supporting his argument for rhymeless quantity with an absolutism so consciously held and explicitly set forth, Campion made the relativism of Daniel's much-praised reply almost inevitable. "Euery language," he observes in the *Defence of Ryme*, "hath her proper number or measure fitted to vse and delight, which Custome, entertaininge by the allowance of the Eare, doth indenize and make naturall." Differences in prosodic fashion arise from "the humour of the Composer and the set of the time." [19]

But Daniel's relativism is more than historical and more than prosodic. He evinces a type of impressionism, a *De gustibus non est disputandum* attitude, frequently condemned as involving a final surrender of the whole critical problem, a denial of the possibility of *any* objective standards, relative or otherwise. His closing phrases lend color to the charge: "we must heerein be content to submit our selues to the law of time, which in few yeeres wil make al that for which we now contend *Nothing.*"

But perhaps because the subsequent course of English poetry has so largely justified his defense of the native tradition, the pervading skepticism of his piece has gone unnoticed. His argument, however, tends to the discrediting not only of quantitative prosody in English but of poetics itself. If this is a minor consideration in judging Daniel's whole achievement in the *Defence,* it is nonetheless of central importance in the history of relativist criticism. Modern absolutists who charge that all relativism ultimately destroys criticism might document their thesis with Daniel's own words:

> Suffer then the world to inioy that which it knowes, and what it likes: Seeing that whatsoeuer force of words doth mooue, delight, and sway the affections of men, in what Scythian sorte soeuer it be disposed or vttered, that is true number, measure, eloquence, and the perfection of speach: which I said hath as many shapes as there be tongues or nations in the world, nor can with all the tyrannicall Rules

of idle Rhetorique be gouerned otherwise then custome and present obseruation will allow.[20]

Even more than Puttenham, Daniel is of course concerned not with the elaboration of a theory but with meeting an attack; as a result, his reasoning displays the *ad hoc* quality common to most Elizabethan criticism. Thus, much of his opposition to Campion's program is grounded on historical relativism. He objects to adopting quantitative numbers "onely to imitate Greekes and Latines, whose felicitie in this kinde might be something to themselues, to whome their owne *idioma* was naturall; but to vs it can yeeld no other commoditie then a sound." Besides, he continues, implicitly denying any intrinsic excellence to the classical system, our admiration for Greek and Roman letters is due to military conquest. But for an accident of history, we might just as well have admired the Welsh and Irish! [21]

Some of his opposition takes the form of the skepticism already noted. Poetry, like other human institutions, is in constant flux; nothing endures. Therefore no rules, certainly no absolute rules, are possible. The wise man conforms to fashion like a good Englishman.[22]

Finally, rhyme is defended on absolutist grounds. Daniel's essay, in fact, illustrates the distinction between historical criticism and critical relativism. To know other times and places (Daniel evidently "knows" even ancient China) is to know that there has been a "variety of ways." And this affords the foundation for his relativism. But Daniel sees rhyme as more than a device peculiarly suited to the English idiom. It is a thing "which both Custome

19

and Nature doth most powerfully defend." "And for our Ryme (which is an excellencie added to this worke of measure, and a Harmonie farre happier than any proportion Antiquitie could euer shew vs) dooth adde more grace, and hath more of delight than euer bare numbers, howsoeuer they can be forced to runne in our slow language, can possibly yeeld." [23] The suggestion here is that the moderns have "improved" poetry by adding one more harmonious element. Rhyme is not merely a compensation for something lost, as it was for Puttenham, because nothing has been lost. The English verse "of measure and accent" is equal to the classical verse "of the number and quantitie of sillables" because both perform the same aesthetic function. The addition of rhyme is therefore a net gain, making modern verse absolutely superior prosodically.

Underlying the praise given Daniel by many modern historians of criticism is an assumption which some critics would challenge: that historical relativist criticism is "better," more "mature" than absolutist criticism. (What this assumption does to the reputations of Aristotle, Coleridge, and Arnold, among others, need not detain us.) Part of the trouble is rooted in the confusion of historical and relativist criticism.

But it also overlooks a second necessary distinction, one which must be made if we are to justify ridiculing the absolutist Thomas Rymer while applauding the just as thoroughly absolutist Coleridge. The distinction is between kinds of absolutism. We may call them monist absolutism and pluralist absolutism; or, avoiding possible misunderstanding, we may adopt the terms "absolutism of means and end" and "absolutism of end." "Means and end" absolutism holds not only that there is one "end" or essential quality in all poetry or in each poetic genre, but that the means of effecting that end are always the same. This principle lies behind much of the Elizabethan prosodic classicism, and it is explicit in the work of Rymer and his contemporaries in the next century.

This discrimination of absolutisms is no mere splitting of hairs. It has a direct bearing on the evaluation of specific works as well as on aesthetic theory. A "means-and-end" absolutist critic of the novel who admired Hardy's work would almost certainly consider Virginia Woolf's beneath critical attention. An "end-only" critic, without adopting relativism, could admire both writers, because "end-only" absolutism sees that the single end, function, or essence which permits grouping widely differing works under the single term *novel* may be achieved in many ways, i.e., by various techniques.[24]

The latter approach is typical of the best nonrelativist criticism of the nineteenth and twentieth centuries. Daniel may therefore be given credit for exemplifying this approach in his little essay, even though it is inconsistent with his skepticism. There is for him an absolute and universal end or function of all poetry, in terms of which he offers a definition: "All verse is but a frame of wordes confined within certaine measure, differing from the ordinarie speach, and introduced, the better to expresse mens conceipts, both for delight and memorie. Which frame of words consisting of *Rithmus* or *Metrum*, Num-

21

ber or measure, are disposed into diuers fashions, according to the humour of the Composer and the set of the time." [25] Whether his definition is acceptable is not in point here. Its significance lies in combining an absolute and universal end for all poetry with a relative means to its attainment. The saving relativism of means is introduced with the final words of the passage: "diuers fashions, according to the humour of the Composer and the set of the time." Daniel saw, as his contemporaries did not, that rhyme and other particulars of versification were not absolutes in the definition of poetry. If the fact seems a truism today, it was not so then or for some time after. The methods involved in this part of his piece anticipate many developed only much later and still reputable today. A recent writer has rightly declared that in "the main body of his actual defence, Daniel had applied sound methods in adopting as his tests those of reason, universality and aesthetic function." [26]

Particularly for the period under consideration, the presence in any critic's work of relativist tendencies bears no necessary relation to its value as criticism. Sidney's wonderful *Apology,* for instance, certainly the brightest ornament of Elizabethan criticism, is largely absolutist, though it contains elements of the historical sense. And it elicited no reply in relativist terms. The same must be said for others, for George Gascoigne and King James on English versification, for E. K. on Spenser's poetic diction, for Nash on Sidney.

## Elizabethan Rudiments

This is natural enough in light of the fact that the critics of this period were engaged by more immediate issues. The question of relative as against absolute criteria is one which they stumble upon, so to speak, in the process of dealing with other matters. Moreover, it is almost entirely in connection with the prosody debate that the issue appears. The disproportionate amount of relativism (and even historical criticism) concerned with verse technique is partly explained by the fact that from Ascham's time "this became, with another less technical one, the main question of Elizabethan criticism. . . ." [27]

There is, however, some protest against a single standard in matters other than versification. Apart from Daniel's sweeping impressionism, a more specific instance is found in Sir John Harington's refusal to accord universal validity to Greek theory and practice in the epic. The ancient rules, he declares, are not properly applicable to *Orlando Furioso*. "But now whereas some will say *Ariosto* wanteth art, reducing all heroicall Poems vnto the methode of *Homer* and certain precepts of *Aristotle,* for Homer I say that that which was commendable in him to write in that age, the times being changed, would be thought otherwise now. . . ." [28] This may be considered a rudimentary form of historical relativism in that it rejects the notion of an absolute standard of judgment. Harington does not, though, apply his principles to the work he is considering. He proceeds to justify Ariosto by showing him like Virgil and true to Aristotle.

Going further, he reveals an element of absolutist historical criticism. Following a comparison of the *Aeneid* and the *Orlando* is the statement that Virgil lacks values he "could not have, for the ignorance of the age he lived in." This ascription of the quality of a work to conditions prevailing during its composition is historical criticism which might have led to a relativist appraisal. But it did not. Harington makes no allowance for the pagan religion of Virgil's time and country. On the contrary, "my author is to be preferred before all the auncient Poets" because they wrote of false, obscene gods.[29] This introduces, in a very crude manner, a moral criterion, as distinct from the strictly formal issues of the prosody quarrel. Whatever its merits, the standard of religious truth is applied to two epics, and applied *absolutely.* Atkins' statement, then, that Harington's remarks show "a maturing of the critical spirit . . . above all, in the claim for the recognition of relative standards in poetry," [30] wants at least the qualification that this relativism did not extend to content.

It remains only to note a passage in Puttenham's *Arte.* In discussing the elusive quality of *decorum,* or "decencie," in speech, he takes the position that there is no fixed rule for determining or detecting it. What is or is not comely is a matter of discretion. "But by reason of the sundry circumstances that mans affaires are, as it were, wrapt in, this *decencie* comes to be very much alterable and subiect to varietie. . . ." [31] The relativism here amounts to the kind of impressionism that involves circular reasoning: good writing is that which is approved by readers of good taste, and good taste consists of appreciating good writing. If this creates more problems than it solves, Puttenham is at least among the first to recognize "graces beyond the reach of art."

Once again, the conclusion seems inescapable that an Elizabethan critic's adoption or rejection of either theoretical position often depended less on settled conviction than on expediency. In defending English poetry, and rhyme, and Ariosto, Puttenham and Daniel and Harington marshalled as many arguments as made for their cases. If they were aware of ultimate logical contradictions, they were with rare exceptions indifferent to them. Lest this seem to derogate from their achievement as a whole, let it be repeated that not until the eighteenth century was there any conscious and systematic attempt to apply the relativist approach to literary evaluation. In now and then glimpsing the principle while busy about other things, the Elizabethans did all we have a right to expect.

# Chapter 3

# Ends and Means

The dependence of neoclassical critical absolutism upon a veneration of the Ancients was slight. Greco-Roman literary precept and practice were honored far less for their antiquity than for their rationally demonstrable truth several decades before Pope wrote that "To copy nature was to copy them." For literary theory in the later seventeenth century was not, as it has sometimes been represented,[1] a perverse exception to the rationalism of the new science. Dryden's critical inconsistencies are not properly explained by saying that he occasionally reacted against the contemporary spirit of rational inquiry in blind deference to authority.[2] His absolutism and his relativism alike are in keeping with the most advanced intellectual attitudes of his day. Undeniably Dryden, like John Dennis and Charles Gildon after him, was critically inconsistent, but not through any kind of intellectual atavism. The inconsistency arose from the very nature of the scientific influence.

Respect for ancient literary achievement there certainly was, but it was a respect based for the most part on a sincere and discerning admiration. Homer and Virgil, Sophocles and Plautus were subjected to an inquiry as thor-

ough and impartial as that applied to classical physics
and medicine. And they stood the test, stood it, for
many critics, far better than their modern counterparts.
To copy their methods, therefore, and to abide by the
critical doctrines laid down by their countrymen seemed
by far the best way to produce good literature.

The great achievements of the age in mathematics were
seen to depend upon the use of the correct method. Bacon
himself, self-styled herald of the new science, had insisted
that the discovery of truth was a matter of applying a
sound method, not the prerogative of individual genius.[3]
In other words, mathematics and the natural sciences were
*arts,* as the term was then used. Was poetry also an art?
Did it too have a body of rules by which to escape from
the morass of opinion and whimsy to the heights of clarity
and precision that were the glory of the sciences? The
very fact of the classical poetics seemed to dictate the
answer: the same nations whose epics and tragedies were,
by almost universal consent, perfect of their kind had
spelled out and passed on the rules of their successful
game. Just as the modern triumphs in science were at-
tributable to the discovery of a method, so were the ancient triumphs in poetry. The Bacons and Descartes'
merely done for natural philosophy what the Aristotles
and the Horaces had done for literature.

Though the assumption involved in this analogy between science and art was repeatedly challenged during
the books quarrel, it lingered as a habit of thought into
the eighteenth century. Leonard Welsted's attack in 1724
indicates the great attraction that the mensurative and

quantitative precision of science had for the neoclassical man of letters. "Could certain Methods be laid down for attaining these Excellencies [of poetry], every one that pleas'd, might be a Poet; as every one that pleases, may be a Geometrician, if he will but have due Patience and Attention. . . ." "It is certain," he admits, that "every Thing depends on Reason"; but he finds it necessary to point out that "it is as certain, that Reason operates differently, when it has different Things for its Object; poetical Reason is not the same as mathematical Reason; there is in good Poetry as rigid Truth, and as essential to the Nature of it, as there is in a Question of *Algebra*, but that Truth is not to be prov'd by the same Process or Way of Working. . . ." [4] But in the seventeenth and early eighteenth centuries this was not the truism it has since become. Their equal treatment by the new Royal Society is evidence of a failure to make a radical distinction between science and art, as Spingarn long ago pointed out.[5] In such circumstances, it is not surprising that the liberalism promised by Daniel's *Defence* failed to materialize.

The rules, then, were poetry's means to its end.[6] Absolutist and relativist, champions of "Ancients" and of "Moderns" alike accepted this principle. Some, however, went further, insisting that a single end necessitated a fixed set of rules. However much this extreme absolutism owed to deference to ancient Greeks and Romans (or to modern Frenchmen), it could and did make an effective appeal to contemporary physical and mathematical science. Thomas Rymer, in 1674, declared the principles of Aristotle's *Poetics* to be as "convincing and clear as any demonstration in *Mathematicks*. 'Tis only needful that we understand them for our consent to the truth of them." [7] "Convincing and clear"—and universally true! For the new science was absolute as well,[8] and therefore magnificently immune to fruitless wrangling.

To admire at once the new science and the old poetics was no paradox. In a century when Englishmen especially were "hot for certainties," when they were weary of the din of debate in politics, religion, and human institutions generally, the imaginative appeal of any discipline that claimed to be systematic and universal must have been great. And it was precisely this quality of independence from opinion that the classical poetics and the new science seemed to possess in common. If it was urged that science could support its claim by its fruits, the absolutist critic pointed to the *Iliad,* to *Oedipus,* to the *Aeneid,* to the *Menaechmi.* This longing to free knowledge from the trammels of controversy helps to explain the fascination that mathematics had for the age and the consequent attempts to apply its unalterable logic to politics, to religion, to morals. In religion it yielded Herbert of Cherbury's *De Veritate* and later Deism. And John Locke thought seriously of placing *"morality amongst the sciences capable of demonstration: wherein I doubt not, but from self-evident propositions, by necessary consequences, as incontestable as those in mathematics, the measures of right and wrong might be* made out, to any one that will apply himself with the same indifferency and attention to the one as he does to the other of those sciences." [9] Why not to aesthetics?

Considered in this light, the truculent tone of the classical absolutists, their manifest hostility to much of the literature and all of the critical bickering of their day, becomes understandable. Even as early as the 1630's Henry Reynolds deplores the "schismes of opinions," and "the almost generall abuse and violence offered to the excellent art of Poesye." Anticipating by some forty-odd years Rymer's use of the term, he displays an impatience with modern critical "Empiricks" that might be felt toward someone who wished to debate the proposition that 2 plus 2 equals 4. The deplorable state of modern poetry was inexcusable when it might easily have been avoided by imitating the Ancients, and "if in this declining state of the world we cannot rectify our oblique one by their perfect and strait line, yet indeavour it. . . ." [10]

A generation later Rymer was more explicit. Poetry's poor showing in contrast to the other "arts" he attributed to the poets' perverse refusal to use the only means calculated to achieve their end. "I therefore made enquiry what *difference* might be in our *Philosophy* and *Manners;* I found that our *Philosophers* agreed well enough with theirs, in the main; however, that our Poets have forc'd another way to the *wood;* a *by-road,* that runs directly cross to that of *Nature, Manners* and *Philosophy* which gain'd the *Ancients* so great veneration." [11] In this passage there is evidence that Rymer pretended to find more agreement between the old and new "philosophies" than actually obtained. But his annoyance with modern poets was not that they did not revere the past, but that they were blind to the obvious.

Jonson, a professed venerator of the classics, had nonetheless a very different attitude toward fixed poetic rules. "For, whereas all other Arts consist of Doctrine, and Precepts: the *Poet* must bee able by nature, and instinct, to powre out the Treasure of his minde. . . ." [12] Mere obscurantism this, to Rymer, whose title page gives notice that he is examining the older tragedy "By the Common sense of all Ages" as well as against ancient practice. Of the two criteria, in fact, the more infallible was this universal good sense, "in the General Notion whereof," as Ferrand Spence typically expressed it in 1686, "every one does agree as much as in the Idea of a Triangle." [13] (The frequency of geometric figures of speech in neoclassical criticism is more than a stylistic fad.) "But if people are prepossest," Rymer protested, "if they will judg of *Rollo* by *Othello,* and one *crooked line* by another, we can never have a certainty." [14]

Thoroughgoing critical absolutism ("absolutism of means and end") persisted well into the eighteenth century. In 1704 Dennis, who had earlier attacked the Rymerian thesis, summed up the logic of this extreme position.

> In short, Poetry is either an Art, or Whimsy and Fanaticism. If it is an Art, it follows that it must propose an End to it self, and afterwards lay down proper Means for the attaining that End: For this is undeniable, that there

31

are proper Means for the attaining of every End, and those Means in Poetry we call the Rules.[15]

And the means are as absolute as the end, for the rules are "both few and short, but eternal and unalterable." [16] Some twenty years later he replies to Welsted's attack on the rules quoted above with the same argument: if poetry is an art it must have rules; these rules must be known and promulgated; the only known rules are those of Aristotle and his interpreters; if this is not so, poetry is not an art (an absurdity).[17] This position is taken by a man whose earlier criticism in opposition to Rymer (e.g., *The Impartial Critick*) employed the historical viewpoint and contained at least the seeds of relativism. If those seeds failed to take root, it was rather because of than in spite of the prevailing climate of opinion.

The work of Gildon took a similarly contradictory course. Scornful of the rules in the last decade of the 1600's, he later became loud in their defense. In Dialogue II of *The Complete Art of Poetry* (1718) he gives explicit formulation to the analogy between mathematically based science and poetics. One of the speakers urges the other to do for criticism what the Newtonians have done for mathematics. Both branches of knowledge are arts: they contemplate ends attainable by a proper methodology. The character Laudon, in fact, charges Sir William Temple with self-contradiction, for Temple in his *Essay on Poetry* had opposed the rules while urging the necessity of "Art." "Now every *Art* in its very Constitution proposes some certain *End* to obtain, and some certain *Means* of obtaining that *End;* but the Means in the

*Art* of *Poetry,* as well as in all others, are what we call the Rules of the *Art.* So that to talk of the Necessity of *Art,* and at the same Time disallow of its *Rules* is downright Nonsense; or the proposing an *End,* without any Means of attaining that *End,* which is equally absurd and ridiculous." [18]

To refute the opponents of the established rules, he continues, it is sufficient to say that poetry is an art that is known, that its rules are those of Aristotle, and "that it is impossible to succeed in this Art by any other Ways." The means are as absolute as the end: ". . . *Poetry* is an Art; for since it has a certain *End,* there must be some certain Way of arriving at that *End.* No Body can doubt of so evident a Truth, that in all Things, where there may be a *Right,* and a *Wrong,* there is an *Art,* and sure Rules to lead you to the former, and direct you how to avoid the latter." Great literature of all ages conforms to these same rules. "For *good Sense,* and *right Reason,* is of all Countries and Places; the Same Subjects, which caus'd so many Tears to be shed in the *Roman Theatre,* produce the same Effect on ours; and those Things, that then gave Distaste do the same now." [19]

To attribute neoclassical critical absolutism to unthinking veneration of the pagan past or timid deference to the French is to confuse cause and effect. It would appear truer to say that the absolutism led to the "enthronement" of the Greek and Roman classics. In Gildon's *Complete Art* the speaker Tyro has been thoroughly convinced of the need for absolute rules when he protests that he sees "no reason why we should be wholly guided by the

Ancients." It is not, he is told, that the moderns are inferior, but that "no Modern has any merit but what he owes to the Rules and Precedents of the *Ancients:* We are asserting the Necessity and Use of the Rules of Art established by the Ancients; and till you have confuted them, what has been said remains in full Force." [20]

They are honored, that is to say, because they have been found irrefutable. This position was of course not original with Gildon. In 1685 Dryden uses the same approach in meeting possible objections to the form and function of opera.

> . . . in order to resolve the problem, this fundamental proposition must be settled, that the first inventors of any art or science, provided they have brought it to perfection, are, in reason, to give laws to it; and, according to their model, all after-undertakers are to build. Thus, in Epic Poetry, no man ought to dispute the authority of Homer, who gave the first being to that masterpiece of art, and endued it with that form of perfection in all its parts that nothing was wanting to its excellency. Virgil therefore, and those very few who have succeeded him, endeavoured not to introduce, or innovate, anything in a design already perfected, but imitated the plan of the inventor; and are only so far true heroic poets as they have built on the foundations of Homer.[21]

The implications of this are clear: if it could be shown that Homer was "imperfect," his method would then have to be rejected. There was only one true method.

For Dryden too the rules were means to an end: ". . . if Nature be to be imitated, then there is a rule for imitating Nature rightly; otherwise there may be an end, and no means conducing to it." [22] And occasionally he saw both means and end as absolutes; in 1695 he wrote that in both painting and poetry the rules were indispensable and unalterable. "This is notoriously true in these two arts; for the way to please being to imitate Nature, both the poets and the painters in ancient times, and in the best ages, have studied her; and from the practice of both these arts the rules have been drawn by which we are instructed how to please, and to compass that end which they obtained, by following their example. For Nature is still the same in all ages, and can never be contrary to herself." [23]

To this extreme absolutism, the opposite of extreme relativism was not the only alternative. A theoretical middle ground exists always, and it was widely adopted in the early neoclassical period by several critics, some of them the very same who sometimes felt impelled to defend the uncompromising absolutism just examined. For this middle position we have suggested the term "absolutism of end": the ends are absolute, but the means to their attainment necessarily vary with changing circumstances. Quite logically, this does not imply an abandonment of rules, does not negate the means-end view, does not, in short, question that literature is an "art." It does insist, however, that no set of rules can be universally and eternally binding, for their efficacy as means to a contemplated end depends upon prevalent conditions of time and place many of which are extra-literary. Frequently this resulted in subjecting the rules to a test essentially pragmatic: only those which perform the job are valid.

Tragedy, for example, always and everywhere involved the purgation of certain emotions; the epic had constantly the aim of inculcating wisdom and virtue by heroic example.[24] But the appeal to the tragic sense in man and his inducement to virtuous emulation could be effected only in consonance with the prepossessions, the hidden premises as it were, of his age and locale: attitudes which are themselves functions of traditional and received political, social, religious, and other institutions. Too often, it is true, these concepts were only vaguely grasped, but occasionally critics were quite explicit.

Sometimes this relativism of means extends only to formal matters, to stylistic details even. Differences among languages, especially, were for a century or more regarded as deterrents to the adoption of classical stylistic devices. Ben Jonson was willing to learn his imagistic techniques from the Romans. "But," he warns, "there are *Hyperboles* which will become one Language, that will by no meanes admit another. . . . Therefore wee must consider in every tongue what is us'd, what receiv'd." [25]

Since hyperboles, like other poetic figures of speech, are valuable only as means of achieving desirable effects, Jonson recognized that the change from Latin to English invalidated certain ancient types. Edward Phillips, in 1675, carried the point further in the preface to his *Theatrum Poetarum* by way of defending the inclusion in his collection of the "uncouth" poets of the Tudor period, whose style and diction were uncongenial to Restoration taste. Nowhere does he suggest a relativist aesthetic as such; "in Arts and Sciences, as well as in Moral Notions," he assures his readers, "I shall not scruple to maintain that what was *verum & bonum* once continues to be so always. . . ." But this is no reason to deny that the fundamental difference between ancient and modern languages requires a different prosodic means of expressing this unalterable *verum & bonum*.

"To the Antient Greecs and Latins, the Modern Poets of all Nations and for several Ages have acknowledged themselves beholding for those, both Precepts and examples, which have been thought conducing to the perfection of Poetry; for the manner of its Garb and dress, which is Vers, we in particular to the *Italians, . . .* the measure of the Greec and Latin Verse being no way suitable to the Modern Languages. . . ." Certain verse forms, Phillips thinks, become one language more than another for certain genres.[26] Thomas Hobbes had thought so too, for he wrote Sir William Davenant that it was the nature of the Greek and Latin languages that made hexametres and quantity "for an Epique Poem most decent . . . ," while in English the most suitable was "the line of ten Syllables, recompencing the neglect of their quantity with the diligence of Rime." [27]

No critic of the period was more drawn to the special problem of language than Dryden himself. On the subject of poetic license in epic poetry he is unwilling to determine how much liberty the poet may take in his use of tropes and figures. "But," he declares, "it is certain that they are to be varied, according to the language

and age in which an author writes. That which would
be allowed to a Grecian poet, Martial tells you, would
not be suffered in a Roman." English, nearer the Latin,
is strict, not free like the Greek. Compound epithets, ele-
gant in the Greek, failed when attempted in English by
Sidney and by Sylvester in his translation of Du Bartas.
And this, he is careful to point out, is a matter rather
"of variety of idiom in languages" than of poetic license.[28] Personal taste or preference, that is, is not the
arbiter here; it is an ineluctible condition imposed by
linguistic peculiarity. Better then for an English poet to
defy the dicta of Aristotle and Longinus concerning
tropes and figures than to write in defiance of his own
medium. For these stylistic devices were merely means
whose value in effecting the desired end was relative,
among other things, to the particular language.

From this viewpoint, the more rigid absolutism of both
end and means becomes not a little ironic: to be true
to these ancient preceptors in little things was to be false
to them in greater. In the next century Edward Young's
*Conjectures on Original Composition* (1759), perhaps the
best known contemporary attack on neoclassical critical
dogmatism, was to bid authors to "imitate not the *Composition,* but the *Man.* For may not this paradox pass
into a maxim? *viz.* 'The less we copy the renowned antients, we shall resemble them the more.' " [29] Some such
maxim might well stand as motto for the absolutist of
end.

The same principle bears directly on the theory of
translation. George Chapman, the translator of Homer,

38

rejecting a word-for-word version as "pedanticall and absurd," considered the translator's art to consist of render-
ing the thoughts of his author in "such a stile and forme
of Oration, as are most apt for the language into which
they are converted." [30] In the verse section of his preface,
he expresses scorn for those translators who

> so much apply
> Their paines and cunnings word for word to render
> Their patient Authors, when they may as well
> Make fish with fowle, Camels with Whales engender,
> Or their tongues speech in other mouths compell.[31]

Careful to claim Horatian authority for his opinion,
Chapman undertook no independent examination of critical theory.

But Dryden did. In considering his contribution, it is
important first to keep in mind that for Dryden, and
perhaps for others in his day, translation was certainly
one form of "imitation," itself a doctrine dependent on
aesthetic absolutism. Imitation, he says, was an invention
of Cowley and Denham. "I take imitation of an author,
in their sense, to be an endeavour of a later poet to
write like one who has written before him, on the same
subject; that is, not to translate his words, or to be confined to his sense, but only to set him as a pattern, and
to write, as he supposes *that author would have done,
had he lived in our age, and in our country.*" This clearly
recognizes that in order to achieve the same end, other
means must be adopted relative to the times. But neither
this method of imitation properly so-called nor metaphrase (word-for-word rendition) appeals to Dryden as

ideal translation. He urges a third method, that of paraphrase (sense-for-sense rendition). For even here, although the poet does not purport to create an original work, metaphrase would defeat the end. Fidelity to his original requires the translator to depart in matters of idiom at least. For "since every language is so full of its own proprieties, that what is beautiful in one, is often barbarous, nay sometimes nonsense, in another, it would be unreasonable to limit a translator to the narrow compass of the author's words: 't is enough if he choose out some expression which does not vitiate the sense. . . ." [32]

The language difference is, in fact, almost an obsession with Dryden,[33] as it was a matter of concern to others. Whenever he speaks of translation, he is almost sure to insist that fidelity of rendition depends largely on stylistic and prosodic adaptations imposed by the language difference. "I cannot boast," he writes in the "Dedication of the Æneis" (1697) with reference to Virgil's exact choice of words,

> that I have been thus exact in my verses; but I have endeavoured to follow the example of my master, and am the first Englishman, perhaps, who made it his design to copy him in his numbers, his choice of words, and his placing them for the sweetness of the sound. On this last consideration I have shunned the *cæsura* as much as possibly I could: for, wherever that is used, it gives a roughness to the verse; of which we can have little need in a language which is overstocked with consonants. Such is not the Latin, where the vowels and consonants are mixed in proportion to each other: yet Virgil judged the vowels to have somewhat of an over-balance, and therefore tempers their sweetness with *cæsuras*. Such difference there is in

tongues, that the same figure, which roughens one, gives majesty to another: and that was it which Virgil studied in his verses.

The end could be reached only by adjusting the prosodic means, by "correcting" for English consonant predominance. Some who reverenced Virgil might object. "Yet," Dryden replies, "I may presume to say . . . that . . . I have endeavoured to make Virgil speak such English as he would himself have spoken, if he had been born in England, and in this present age." [34]

Thus, the absolutist of end saw such dictional and prosodic means as variable with factors other than mere idiomatic and linguistic differences between one culture and another; nor was relativism of means confined to stylistic matters. Ben Jonson, referring to his violation of the rules of unity of time and the use of a chorus in his tragedy *Sejanus,* declared that he knew no modern who had been able to follow these rules successfully. "Nor is it needful," he adds, "or almost possible, in these our Times, and to such Auditors as commonly Things are presented, to obserue the ould state and splendour of *Drammatick Poëmes,* with preseruation of any popular delight." Jonson gives no suggestion that the essential nature of tragedy can change. He argues only that the efficacy of certain formal characteristics depends on the time and place of presentation. He thus asks his reader to pardon him "the absence of these *Formes"* since "in truth of Argument, dignity of Persons, gravity and height of Elocution, fulnesse and frequencie of Sentence, I have discharg'd the other offices of a *Tragick* writer. . . ." [35]

41

It is notable that Jonson's remarks are more an apology for necessary lapses from the classical way than a general statement of relativist principle.

Later in the century Dryden could be bolder. In *An Essay of Dramatic Poesy* (1668), Crites, defending the ancient drama against Eugenius' championship of the modern, rejects his opponent's belief that the arts progress. But he does admit that they change, and that therefore an ancient poet, "had he lived in our age . . . had altered many things; not that they were not as natural before, but that he might accommodate himself to the age he lived in." [36] Here, in one of the earliest of the poet's critical pieces, we have at least a general recognition of a relationship between the character of a literary work and the time of its composition. No specific application of the principle is attempted, though the context suggests that Crites is thinking of an alteration in comparatively minor matters (means), not in the whole design and purpose (end) of the drama.

Dryden's brother-in-law, Sir Robert Howard, does afford a most interesting illustration of the dependence of dramatic method upon prevalent circumstances, in this case the larger context of the literary tradition. "The manner of the Stage-Entertainments," he writes, "have differ'd in all Ages. . . ." He defends his own departures from such ancient devices as the chorus and the *nuntius* while blaming the French for retaining them. For such usages, he reasons, were dictated by the traditional dramatic subjects, which contained violent and supernatural elements (e.g., Medea's magic cauldron) whose visible representation would have made them either repulsive or incredible. And he quotes Horace's *incredulus odi* in support. "So that it appears a fault to chuse such Subjects for the Stage, but much greater to affect that Method which those Subjects enforce; and therefore the *French* seem much mistaken, who without the necessity sometimes commit the Error. . . ." [37]

The question is even more searchingly defined in Dryden's regrettably unelaborated "Heads of an Answer" to Rymer's *Tragedies of the Last Age* (1678). In the first place, the underlying pragmatism of relativism of means is clearly revealed. Rymer had argued that the popularity of the older English tragedies merely testified to the depravity of the public taste. "If he urge," Dryden retorts, "that the general taste is depraved his arguments to prove this can at best but evince that our poets took *not the best way* to raise those passions; but experience proves against him, that *these means,* which they have used, have been successful, and have produced them." The argument of success, especially forceful perhaps to a practicing playwright like Dryden, seemed to him reason for questioning Rymer's literal insistence on minor matters, a questioning that forbade his accepting the conclusion that modern taste was perverted. "And one reason of that success is, in my opinion, this, that Shakespeare and Fletcher have written to the genius of the age and nation in which they lived; for though nature, as he [Rymer] objects, is the same in all places, and reason too the same, yet the climate, the age, the disposition of the people, to whom

43

a poet writes, may be so different that what pleased the Greeks would not satisfy an English audience."

This is no mere defense of the moderns. Dryden is not even denying that the Greek work was better. For he immediately grants that "if they [the Greeks] proceeded upon a foundation of truer reason to please the Athenians than Shakespeare and Fletcher to please the English, it only shews that the Athenians were a more judicious people; but the poet's business is certainly to please the audience." [38] This is going far to be fair, farther than complete relativism would have allowed. But Dryden is not here questioning ends, only means. Grant what you will as to the superiority of Athenian taste, "the poet's business is certainly to please the audience," not as an end in itself but as the condition *sine qua non* of achieving any end at all.

Dryden raises and answers the question again on the subject of criticism of tragedy. The preface to *Troilus and Cressida* reveals his conviction that the essentials of the tragic form were established for all time by the Ancients. To what extent, he asks, ought a modern playwright to imitate the plots of Shakespeare and Fletcher, and answers "that we ought to follow them so far only as they have copied the excellencies of those who invented and *brought to perfection* Dramatic Poetry. . . ." No relativist of means and end both would have used the words here italicized. But no absolutist of means would have added, as Dryden does, "those things only excepted, which religion, custom of countries, idioms of languages, etc., have altered in the *superstructures,* but

44

not in the *foundation* of the design." [39] The words *super-structures* and *foundation* convey nicely the distinction upon which the absolutist of end based the limitation of his absolutism. It is not too much to say that Rymer's great fault lay in his apparent inability to recognize it, whereas Dryden had done so as early as 1668. In his "Defence of an Essay" he remarks of Howard's attack on the dramatic rules "that he has mistaken the foundation for that which is built upon it. . . ." and (sarcastically) that "he has only made a small mistake, of the means conducing to the end for the end itself, and of the super-structure for the foundation. . . ." [40]

Obvious, and often disturbing, to many seventeenth century writers was the effect of one great cultural change upon epic theory and practice: the change from paganism to Christianity. Several conclusions were reached both before and after Milton's triumphant demonstration (often blandly overlooked). But for some the religious change from ancient to modern times did not alter the fundamental form and function of the epic genre. It involved only an adaptation of the means, in this case the religious content. Sir William Davenant believed that his heroic poem shared with Homer's and Virgil's the end of teaching virtue and good manners. But to follow their guidance to the extent of the religious setting would, he felt, militate against that end: "My Argument I resolv'd should consist of Christian persons; for since religion doth generally beget and govern manners, I thought the example of their actions would prevail most upon our

own by being deriv'd from the same doctrin and authority. . . ." [41]

The position (or rather various positions) assumed by
the "school of taste" calls for more careful analysis than
it has generally received. The word "taste" itself often
bears more than one meaning and thus may fall into the
context of more than one critical theory even within the
work of a single critic. Dryden appears to be a case in
point. One meaning that the word bore for him, however, is clear enough, and it must be considered a rela-
tivistic element in his criticism. No rule or body of rules,
he felt, that made no allowance for contemporary literary
taste was satisfactory. Both his knowledge of literary history and his experience as poet and playwright contributed to the conviction expressed in the opening lines of
the "Epilogue" to the second part of *The Conquest of
Granada* (1672):

> They, who have best succeeded on the stage
> Have still conform'd their genius to their age.[42]

In this piece, as occasionally elsewhere, Dryden apparently subscribes to a belief in a progress of taste induc-
ing the flattering assurance that he and his contemporaries belonged to "an age more gallant than the last."
Elsewhere still, however, and in more sober passages of
his critical writing, it becomes clear that what he sees
is change rather than (necessarily) improvement. Defending Persius and Juvenal for having abandoned Horace's
rude, colloquial style in their satire, he asks, "Has not
Virgil changed the manner of Homer's heroes in his

46

*Æneis?* Certainly he has, and for the better: for Virgil's age was more civilised, and better bred; and he writ according to the politeness of Rome, under the reign of Augustus Caesar, not to the rudeness of Agamemnon's age, or the times of Homer. Why should we offer to confine free spirits to one form, when we cannot so much as confine our bodies to one fashion of apparel?"

Donne's satires, he continues, for all their wit, suffer from too slavish adherence to the Horatian manner; "and I may safely say it of this present age, that if we are not so great wits as Donne, yet certainly we are better poets." [43] Presumably, they were "better" poets in that they wrote with an eye to current taste. Dryden's meaning is somewhat obscure. But his objection seems to be that Donne simply parodied Horace in English, whereas his proper task was to make the Roman "speak such English as he would himself have spoken, if he had been born in England" and in Donne's age.

John Dennis, untroubled perhaps by Dryden's virtues of diffidence and skepticism, made an even bolder case for relativism of means, notably in Dialogue IV of *The Impartial Critick* (1693). "Now then," says Beaumont to Freeman,

> let me hear your Objections to Mr. *Rymer's* Design; for nothing can seem more commendable to me, than his intention, which is to restore Tragedy to its primitive purity, by re-establishing the Ancient Method, and reviving the Rules of *Aristotle*.
>
> *Freem.* I am for observing the Rules of *Aristotle,* as much as any Man living, as far as it can be done without re-establishing the Ancient Method. [44]

47

## Ends and Means

The phrases "the Rules of Aristotle" and "the Ancient Method" are roughly synonymous with Dryden's *foundation* and *superstructures,* respectively, the first having to do with the unchanging function of the tragic form, the second with those means to its implementation which are subject to "historical" variation.

Going no further than it did, this approach obviously involved no wholesale rejection of Aristotle. It did, however, amount to a more responsible reading of the *Poetics* which attempted to discriminate between those parts of it which were "for all time" and those which were perishable. Charles Gildon echoes this view (as he echoes so many others elsewhere) by way of attacking the "Ancients." The enemies of the moderns, he tells a friend,

> deny them to be Poets because they have not strictly observed the Rules laid down by *Aristotle,* but by that they discover themselves either ignorant or negligent of the most chief and important end of Poetry, that is, Pleasure. Now, it cannot be deny'd but he is the best Poet who takes the surest means to obtain the end he aims at; in which, regard must be had to the *Humour, Custom,* and *Inclination* of the Auditory; but an *English* Audience will never be pleas'd with a dry, Jejune and formal Method [that] excludes Variety as the Religious observation of the Rules of *Aristotle* does.[45]

The line between relativism of means and radical relativism is frequently hard to draw. Analysis of the critical thought of this or any period risks distortion whenever it neglects frankly to recognize the general failure of any critical position to fall neatly and exclusively into one theoretical category. Add to this the frequency with

48

which a single critic may at different times of his career occupy different and even antithetical positions. Such complexities warn against generalizations which attempt to label any critics except those at either extreme of the scale.

Nonetheless, the process of analysis itself reveals the weakness of other generalizations. "The recognition of the relationship between literature and its cultural background," one scholar has concluded, "was the most important mark of historical criticism, for when this is admitted the critic, whose views are conditioned by diverse geographical, racial, and social factors, must admit the impossibility of an absolute judgment of value." [46] The fact is, however, that the type of critic here referred to frequently made no such admission. More important, a recognition of the existence and an understanding of the nature of relativism of means reveal that he was not logically bound to do so.

# Chapter 4

# Relativism of Ends

Of the more liberal absolutism (of end)—an effective compromise between the extremes of two critical methods —much can be written. Its record, even within the period covered by this book, is quite full, and in succeeding ages it becomes the dominant type, embraced by most of those whom we consider leading critics. It has been expounded in theory and widely and brilliantly applied to poetry, drama, and prose fiction.

In contrast, the method of relativist appraisal, even in our own day, has received little theoretical elaboration and less direct application. As Frederick Pottle finds only absolutists among traditional English critics, so Herbert J. Muller can discover among the diversified critical "schools" of recent years almost everything but relativism.[1] In the era we are considering it is almost entirely negative, a protest against some absolutism. At no time have its supporters constructed a system by which their varying yardstick may be applied. They have advanced two principal arguments: the plea that such-a-work should be judged not by prederived criteria but by laws properly applicable to it; and the proposition that, each separate work being unique, its value was a matter of individual taste. The exponents of both these views have had the advantage of freeing themselves from the tyranny of rigid systems. The first group, moreover, could gain conviction by pointing to numerous instances of the misapplication of dogmatic rules to a given work. The second, which gained wide currency at the end of the last century, has profited by its stress on two undoubted truths: no two art products, like no two human beings, are ever entirely alike, and no two persons can ever respond in quite the same way to the same art product.

Despite these advantages, relativism has been far less fruitful than absolutism. Writers who have held that the work of each age must be judged by standards other than those proper to other ages or cultures have largely failed to demonstrate how we can know what the standards are in each case. Their method is at best highly complex. Granted that we must study the institutional context of early eighteenth century England before we dare judge Pope's achievement, can such study ever restore the "feeling" of readers of that day? Can we, even for a moment, cease to respond to some extent as twentieth century Americans? In any event this view would argue that each age could best judge its own production. It would say, for example, that Emily Brontë's *Wuthering Heights* is a minor novel, not the classic or near-classic modern critics have declared it to be. There is general agreement that critics should employ a "varying yardstick"; there seems almost no agreement as to where the yardstick must be "set" for a given measuring job. "So far as art depends on culture and not upon instinct," Stephen

C. Pepper writes, "the art of one age cannot be vividly repeated in another, and, if the art of an earlier age appeals to a later, it is often for other than the original reasons, so that as contextualists repeat, sometimes too insistently, critics are required in each age to register the aesthetic judgments of that age." [2]

Relativists of the second type, the impressionists or subjectivists, deny the possibility of any objective standards. Their work is thus a series of "appreciations," which, as they sometimes admit, come nearer to being spiritual autobiographies by the critics than judicial analyses of a work or author.[3] For these reasons, among others, we cannot expect to find in the seventeenth and early eighteenth centuries more than a smattering of what we have called relativism of ends. It is fair to say with one scholar that "the principle of relativity was frequently discussed" from 1660 to 1700, but not developed until the later eighteenth and nineteenth centuries.[4] Still, what there was is important apart from its role in the early history of English relativist criticism. An examination of its nature and its ideational sources is indispensable to any comprehension of the continuing debate between relativist and absolutist.

The most considered relativist expression is to be found in the writings of those few critics who undertook rejoinders to Thomas Rymer's *Tragedies of the Last Age* (1678) and *Short View of Tragedy* (1692). Widely read, Rymer's books performed a noteworthy service to the de-

velopment of English literary criticism. By propounding
the absolutist position in an extreme form, they drove
dissenting critics to re-examine the theoretical bases of
appraisal. Incontrovertible on his own premises, Rymer
forced his opponents to scrutinize the premises themselves. The result was salutary; to this "worst critic that
ever lived" we are at least indebted for considerable clar-
ification of a fundamental issue.

In much of Dryden's "Heads of an Answer to Rymer,"
the poet is content to question only the means to the end
of tragedy. Rymer could be answered, Dryden thought, by
granting that the Greek way to the end of tragedy ("to
cause pity and terror") was better *for Greeks,* while insisting that another way would better conduce to the
same end *for Englishmen.* But his speculation did not
stop there. Another possible refutation, he continues,
should prove "That other ends as suitable to the nature
of tragedy may be found in the English, which were not
in the Greek." It is clear from the "Heads" that Dryden
was wavering between relativism of means and aesthetic
pluralism. Further on, after repeating his mild objection
that "the English way" is, for the English, just as pro-
ductive of pity and terror, he adds (as though suddenly
thinking better of it): "And if we should grant that the
Greeks performed this better, perhaps it may admit of
dispute whether pity and terror are either the prime, or
at least the only ends of tragedy." [5]

Had Dryden "worked these 'Heads' out," Saintsbury
wrote, "he might have solved the whole mystery of criticism as far as in all probability it ever can be solved, or

53

at the very least as far as it could be solved with the knowledge of literature at his disposal." [6] Whatever reservations one might wish to make to this judgment, it is eloquent testimony to the clarity and catholicity of Dryden's critical thinking. Obviously that thinking was not "thought through"; it is tentative, provisional, inconsistent. There are verbal illogicalities at which one may, with intellectual hindsight, easily cavil. Does the phrase *"other ends* as suitable to the nature of tragedy" not beg the question, for example, since it is precisely the "nature" of tragedy which is at issue? The last passage quoted contains the germ of two quite separate (and antithetical) theories. The notion that terror and pity are not the "prime" ends of tragedy suggests a new absolutism; whereas the notion that they are not "the only ends" leads to relativism. And so forth. Yet it seems only fair to point out that if Dryden missed the chance to "solve the whole mystery of criticism," no one seems to have done so since. Moreover, the particular "mystery" that concerns us here is no nearer solution after almost two centuries, except as it is discovered to be far more complex than Dryden seems to have suspected.

St. Évremond, the brilliant French émigré who so profoundly affected seventeenth century English critical thought, declared unreservedly that each literary era constructed its own aesthetic. "It must be acknowledg'd that *Aristotle's* ART of POETRY is an excellent Piece of Work: But however there's nothing so perfect in it, as to be the standing Rule of all Nations, and all Ages." Just as modern philosophers and scientists have had to reject much of his work in their fields, so "our Poets have spy'd out *Faults* in his POETICKS, at least with respect to Us. . . ." [7]

Notable among Englishmen influenced by St. Évremond was John Dennis. *The Impartial Critick: or, Some Observations Upon a Late Book, Entituled, A Short View of Tragedy, Written by Mr. Rymer* (1693) offers a relativist counterargument to Rymer's later book in terms less diffident and more specific than Dryden's against the earlier. A passage from the prefatory letter, much noticed and praised, is pertinent here.

> For to set up the *Grecian* Method amongst us with success, it is absolutely necessary to restore not only their Religion and their Polity, but to transport us to the same Climate in which *Sophocles* and *Euripides* writ; or else by reason of those different Circumstances, several things which were graceful and decent with them, must seem ridiculous and absurd to us, as several things which would have appear'd highly extravagant to them, must look proper and becoming with us.

It is hard to find a more succinct statement of the case for historical relativism. Better still, Dennis offers supporting illustrations. As examples of ancient tragic elements no longer acceptable, he mentions one of form, the chorus, and one of content, the lament of Sophocles' Antigone that she must die a virgin. As a modern tragic element that would have been "highly extravagant" to the Greeks, he instances the love theme (to which Rymer had objected), explaining the innovation on the grounds of the difference between the Greek and English climates. In the warmer Mediterranean, we are told, love was to

55

be instinctively indulged in, not written or even talked about.[8] However dubious and even amusing [9] such reasoning may appear today, it has the merit of consistency with his theory.

Dennis' position here implies much more than the limited relativism elsewhere in this same essay. It suggests, for instance, a relativism so complete as to render the literature of one culture largely incomprehensible to any other culture sufficiently divergent. Pushed to its logical conclusion, his thesis raises the somewhat depressing prospect of a cultural discontinuity allowing even the greatest works a vitality enduring only in proportion as subsequent civilizations shall resemble that which produced them.[10] Certainly it makes mockery of Shakespeare's boast in Sonnet LV and Horace's confident *Exegi monumentum aere perennius.*

But Dennis did not—doubtless in his day could not—see the consequences of his fundamental premise. Indeed the conclusions he draws from it in this very essay do not exactly square, for as the discussion progresses Freeman (i.e., Dennis) takes a gradually more conservative stand. In Dialogue II, for instance, he gives expression to the thoroughly relativist idea that each age must have its own poetic. Beaumont and Freeman have been discussing Aristotle's rules and modern English tragedy.

> *Beaum.* Do you believe then, that *Aristotle,* if he could rise again, would condemn our *English Oedipus?*

> *Freem.* He would condemn it, or he would be forc'd to recede from his own Principles. . . .[11]

# Relativism of Ends

But by Dialogue IV, as we have seen, Freeman has retreated to a position that makes a distinction between "the Rules of Aristotle" and "the Ancient Method," thus limiting his relativism to the means.

We need not pursue the shifts of ground almost inevitable at this early period in the history of modern critical theory. Far more significant and influential in that history was Dennis' persistence in the concept of change and its relation to questions of literary taste and standards. In a critique of Sir Richard Blackmore's *Prince Arthur* he applies it to epic theory. Granting that episodes are essential to epic structure, he asks "whether some Episodes, which do not in the least offend against Probability or Reason in *Virgil,* may not be reasonably suppos'd to be highly improbable, when they are copied in a modern Poem, by a Poet of our Age, by reason of the vastly different Circumstances of Times, Places, Persons, Customs, Religions, and common received Opinions." [12]

Dennis does not elucidate. But a few years later, in a passage which suggests that he was ahead of his contemporaries in recognizing the complexities of the issue, he touches upon a problem, still unresolved, that arises in consequence of the relativist premise. Homer, he argues, is inferior to Virgil because of his extravagant theology. But not absolutely.

> And, therefore when I say, that *Virgil* is to be preferr'd to *Homer,* I mean, that he is so in regard to us, because he is capable of giving us a greater Pleasure than *Homer;* but I do not pretend at the same Time, that *Virgil* is ca-

pable of giving us a greater Pleasure than *Homer* gave his Contemporaries. As likewise when I affirm, that the Moderns, by joining Poetry with the True Religion, will have the Advantage of the Ancients, I mean only in regard to us, to whom they will give a greater Pleasure than the Ancients can do, but not a greater than the Ancients gave their Contemporaries.[13]

The problem here glimpsed is in a sense a by-product of relativist criticism: for even when relative criteria have been used in judging a literary work, is it possible for readers to appreciate the work fully? If not, as Dennis here declares, then surely any work has only a temporary value. But value is the very thing criteria are supposed to measure. And so on in a circle difficult to break except by the doubtful conclusion that critics are able to render accurate value judgments on books they do not enjoy reading. Neither space nor our purpose permits further discussion of this dilemma here. Suffice it to say that Dennis was later to solve it—but only by abandoning relativism for a new absolutism!

Gildon too had his fling at Rymer, in a book of essays published in 1694. In a defense of Shakespeare in which he refers with approval to Dennis' *Impartial Critick,* Gildon argues that the critical dogmas of Rapin, Bossu, and Dacier, which Rymer had used, are misapplied to Shakespeare. Although he fails to develop it, this of course is an argument for relative standards of appraisal. He is openly contemptuous of Rymer's ranking Shakespeare "in a Class below *Sternold* or *Flecknoe* . . . because he has not come close to the Rules *Aristotle* drew from the Practice of the *Greek* Poets. . . ."

## Relativism of Ends

Like Dennis, he refutes Rymer's defense of the chorus by showing that it is not an essential of tragedy. At first glance this would appear to be relativism of means, implying that *all* tragedies share the same essentials. But for Gildon modern tragedy is evidently radically different from the old. When tragedy became secular, he writes, the chorus lost its function, the praise of Bacchus. "The End therefore and Aim of it being thus alter'd, the Mediums to that *End,* must of Consequence, be alter'd too." Again as with Dennis, Gildon's historical view is backed by illustrative examples. The prospect of the fall of a prince, he says, was more moving to Athenian audiences than to English because the latter, having experienced it in history, found it far less awesome on the stage.[14]

Finally, Gildon reveals with special clarity how the quarrel between "Ancients" and "Moderns" often turned upon a theoretical disagreement between absolutist and relativist. He takes the trouble to quote a long passage from Rapin's *Réflexions sur la Poétique d'Aristote* (translated by Rymer in 1674). The French critic, regretfully admitting that the French national temper and taste favored love in tragedy, had insisted nonetheless that it derogated from the dignity of a genre whose proper passions were terror and pity. As to the national temper, Gildon replies, it argues *for* deviating from ancient practice, "for which he gives so good Reasons, that 'twould have been a madness not to have form'd a new System, since the Genius, the Character, Humour and Manners of the People, requir'd as much." [15] For Rapin (and Rymer) French taste was wrong by the test of an aesthetic immutable because independent of the temporal and local milieu; for Gildon, since he regarded any aesthetic system as a function of that milieu, such a conclusion was impossible.

To the comic dramatist George Farquhar it was absurd. He asks "by what Authority shou'd *Aristotle*'s Rules of Poetry stand so fixt and immutable?" and answers, with triumphant sarcasm,

> Why, by the Authority of two Thousand Years standing, because thro' this long Revolution of time the World has still continu'd the same—By the Authority of their being receiv'd at *Athens,* a City, the very same with *London* in every particular; their Habits the same, the Humours [16] alike, their publick Transactions and private Societies *Alamode France;* in short, so very much the same in every Circumstance, that *Aristotle*'s Criticisms may give rules to *Drury Lane;* the *Areopagus* give judgment upon a Case in the *Kings Bench,* and old *Solon* shall give Laws to the *House of Commons.*[17]

This is no limited relativism, but a thoroughgoing rejection of the old. Despite the flippancy of his tone, Farquhar is not unwilling to examine his ground logically. Borrowing the *utile-dulce* theory of comedy and the dialectic of means and ends, he concludes that,

> without all Dispute, whatever means are most proper and expedient for compassing this End and Intention, they must be the *just Rules* of *Comedy,* and the *true Art of the Stage.*
>
> We must consider then, in the first place, that our Business lies not with a *French* or a *Spanish* Audience; that our Design is not to hold forth to ancient *Greece,* nor to

# Relativism of Ends

moralize upon the Vices and Defaults of the *Roman* Commonwealth: No, no—An English Play is intended for the Use and Instruction an English Audience, a People not only separated from the rest of the World by Situation, but different also from other Nations as well in the Complexion and Temperament of the Natural Body, as in the Constitution of our Body Politick: As we are a Mixture of many Nations, so we have the most unaccountable Medley of Humours among us of any People upon Earth; these Humours produced Variety of Follies, some of 'um unknown to former Ages; these new Distempers must have new Remedies, which are nothing but new Counsels and Instructions.

That his relativism is of the end as well as the means he removes all doubt by adding: "Now, Sir, if our *Utile,* which is the End, be different from the Ancients, pray let our *Dulce,* which is the Means, be so too. . . ." Farquhar's relativism, too, is ultimately pragmatic. The criterion, he insists, is what works with an English audience. And he therefore advises his fellow dramatists to study not Greek plays, but those of Shakespeare, Jonson, and Fletcher. From these they must derive the rules of their craft.[18]

If relativism did not come into its own until quite late in the eighteenth century, it did have its pioneers earlier. Even many critics whose main position was absolutist made concessions to relativism or felt impelled by its growing currency to relax their theoretical rigidity. Thomas Purney, for instance, writing on the pastoral form in terms predominantly absolutist, concedes that several sorts of "tempers" and "geniuses" may support as many kinds of writings. His essay, in sum, outlines what he considers the best type of pastoral, but his concession as to other possible types attests to a remarkable degree of aesthetic tolerance. He would not rob anyone of taking pleasure in "what is not really pleasant." If there is "a Method . . . still more delightful, the Critick is to be observed who points out the Way thereto." Thus, he continues, if some people like Theocritus and Virgil, then there may be "several sorts of Pastorals." And he is even more generous with tragedy and epic: *Julius Caesar* and *The Orphan* are of "different sorts"; Milton and Homer "as different as *East* and *West,* yet both excellent." [19]

So far we have examined only one of the two main types of relativism. There remains the view that the only possible measure of artistic value is taste, which is unaccountable, irreducible to an objective system, and unpredictable. It had long been for obvious reasons a notion attractive to practicing poets, and it is hard to know when it was sincerely held and when it was used as a convenient defense against critical attack. "Taste," however, was a complex word. It meant sometimes individual taste, sometimes popular predilection: it could take the form "I like such-and-such" or "People nowadays like such-and-such." The common feature was its lawlessness, its ultimate negation of all critical systems. It was destructive rather than constructive.

Sir Robert Howard, confessing his inability to please current taste, would not arraign that taste. "I rather," he wrote, "blame the unnecessary understanding of some that have labour'd to give strict rules to things that are not Mathematical . . . for in the difference of *Tragedy* and *Comedy,* and of *Fars* it self, there can be no determination but by the Taste; nor in the manner of their Composure. . . ." [20] Dryden's rejoinder makes clear his own rejection of subjective relativism. "The liking or disliking of the people gives the play the denomination of good or bad, but does not really make or constitute it such." Bound as poet to delight his audience, he himself is writing comedies in compliance to current public preference; "but it does not follow for that reason, that Comedy is to be preferred before Tragedy in its own nature. . . ." [21] To say that "there can be no determination but by the Taste" is almost tantamount to saying that there can be no determination at all. Ultimately, it removes the critical problem from the nature of the work to the psychological make-up of the reader.

Clarence De Witt Thorpe finds in Hobbes' *Leviathan* the notion of "subjective, and, incidentally, relative, standards in taste and morals. . . . That delight, or the sense of beauty, should be regarded as not only subjective but relative, depending on individual reactions which in turn are governed by individual experiences, is inherent in Hobbes's philosophical conceptions. . . . Individual reactions, then, cannot be referred to any set standards." [22] This individualist subjectivism, despite Hobbes' great reputation, seems not to have become a distinct critical theory in the period under consideration. Rather, it was absorbed into the more characteristic skepticism of the age, an intellectual ingredient which flavored the thinking even of Dryden himself,[23] and took the form of a sophisticated Pyrhonnism. At best it made men distrustful of absolutes; at worst it made them despair of any certainties. A passage in Sir William Temple's *On Ancient and Modern Learning* (1690) accurately typifies this attitude. Man, Temple wrote, is naturally inclined to take his opinions for truth: ". . . nay, though his Opinions change every Week or every Day, yet he is sure, or at least confident, that his present thoughts and conclusions are just and true, and cannot be deceived. . . ." Among many miseries, man "has this one Felicity to Comfort and Support him, That in all ages, in all things, every man is always in the right." [24]

Among other reasons why the notion of taste was a minor thread in the fabric of relativism is that it equally well supports absolutism.[25] Taste, though incapable of systematic analysis, need not be individual. The elusive something could be regarded, and was regarded by some, as a *common* psychological factor; according to this conception, all men of good taste would intuitively arrive at the same judgment of the same literary work. Aesthetic values, the elements to which this universal intuition responded, were thus absolute. Used first as a relativist weapon, "taste" was later captured and more effectively used by the opposite camp. Thus with Temple, as one scholar has noted, it was part of the relativism of the age. "Gradually, however, the encroachment of rationalism on the individualism of the School of Taste began; instead of an essentially personal instinct, taste came to be looked upon as an absolute standard, just as fixed and immutable as reason itself." [26] In sum, then, "lawless" relativism has little or no history worth recording in this period. For the relativists found it to be a weapon defensive at best, double-edged at worst.

Despite their paucity, the specific applications of the relative method to the appraisal of works and authors are worth examination. As might be expected, they tend to alter the traditional judgments. Gildon, for instance, finds that Homer has received more credit than he deserves. Alluding to Rapin's praise of the Greek poet's variety of "numbers," he protests that the prosodic beauty is a "property of the *Greek* Language, which makes it the easier Task for *Homer* to perform, and by consequence, lessens his merit on that Account." It is therefore a false judgment to rate Homer a better metrist than Virgil, for the Roman has as much of this variety "as the *Roman* Language wou'd allow. . . ." [27] Here the relative factor, the nature of the language, requires that the yardstick for measuring prosodic achievement be shorter for a Latin than for a Greek poet.

What is perhaps a more objectionable type of relativism results when the current taste is uncritically accepted as the standard. Good authors may be "scaled down" or neglected only because temporarily out of vogue. An interesting instance is the fate of Chaucer, Spenser, and Shakespeare at the hands of Edward Bysshe. In *The Art of English Poetry* (1702), he tells his readers, he has generally avoided quotation of these three poets despite their intrinsic merits, because "their Language is now become so antiquated and obsolete, that most Readers of our Age have no Ear for them: And this is the Reason that the good Shakespeare himself is not so frequently cited in this Collection, as he would otherwise deserve to be." [28] Considering his purpose, which was to set before English readers examples of the best English poetry, this is curious reasoning.

John Oldmixon's historical criticism is sounder. He applies it in defense of a poem of his own, in which, contrary to the rule, he had used the pastoral form for a "heroic" subject. Citing Virgil's similar usage in the *Eclogues,* Oldmixon proceeds to justify it by bringing history to bear on literary judgment. "The Shepherds in those Days had not only the Charge of their Flocks upon their Hands, but the Care of the State; and as the Riches of the World consisted chiefly in the Riches of the Field, Flocks, Herds and Corn; so Husbandry and Labour were so far from being thought below Persons of the highest Quality, that Kings held at once the Crook and the Scepter. . . ." [29] This is a good example of applied historical relativism, for Oldmixon undertakes to explain and *defend* genre content in terms of historical conditions. Ignorance of these conditions would cause unfair censure of Virgil.

Better known is John Hughes' perceptive "Remarks on the Faërie Queene" in his 1715 edition of Spenser. His approach exemplifies that characteristic of historical criticism by which the critic attempts first to account causally for the work before him. Thus Spenser's loose structure he imputes to his reading of the modern Italians and to the particular bent of his genius. Crude in their over-simplification, these notions nonetheless foreshadowed the whole development of literary biography and led logically though perhaps regrettably to the Romantic and post-Romantic extreme of regarding a literary work as primarily an expression of personality.

Hughes' criticism is relativist as well as historical. He admits immediately that Spenser's poem does not accord with "the Rules of Epick Poetry, as they have been drawn from the Practice of *Homer* and *Virgil*." Indeed, by such conventional standards "the whole Frame of it wou'd appear monstrous. . . . But as it is plain the Author never design'd it by those Rules," Hughes argues for considering it a *different kind* of poem. It is not a question of applying the rules with historical allowances. They are simply irrelevant to *The Faërie Queene,* for "to compare it . . . with the Models of Antiquity, wou'd be like drawing a Parallel between the *Roman* and the *Gothick* Architecture." [30]

Hughes' defense of Spenser's art is based exclusively on his historical relativism. The fact is worth noting because so many critics, having defended an author in relativist terms, found it difficult to resist the temptation to declare his absolute superiority as well. In 1722, Sir Richard Steele, seeking probably to prepare English taste for his forthcoming *The Conscious Lovers,* attacked the Restoration comic mode in a series of articles in the *Theatre.* Steele found fault especially with the "fine gentleman" of the Restoration stage, as typified by Etherege's Sir Fopling Flutter. In the rejoinder published in the same year by John Dennis the argument is on the question of what constitutes "genteel" comedy. Dennis is not quite ready to grant that Etherege intended such. "But if Sir *George* did design to make it a genteel one, he was oblig'd to adapt it to that Notion of Gentility, which he knew very well, that the World at that Time had, and we see he succeeded accordingly." This is a perfectly acceptable relativist defense of Restoration stage immorality still used today. Dennis, however, saw fit to shift his ground and defend the earlier comic manner in absolute terms: comedy is designed to arouse laughter, not tears.[31]

From all the evidence, one conclusion at least can be safely drawn. The *idea* of a relativist aesthetic was grasped and enunciated decades before it was consistently applied. Aside from the reasons for this already given, it may be added that the neoclassical absolutes, powerful deterrents to the relativist tendency, thoroughly permeated the thinking of the relativists themselves. Thomas Blackwell, who in 1735 published the first full-length examination of Homer from the point of view of historical relativism, concluded that Homer's genius had been over-rated, "That his *Good Fortune* was far Superiour to his *Skill*." Yet he could also find in the "Tales that raise our Wonder in the *Odyssey*" that "that same *Simplicity* has been preserved in the Relation, and has accomodated them to the Understanding of all Ranks of Men. It was this happy Circumstance that directed the Poet . . . to touch the *Universal Ear* so just and true, that no change of Manners or Politicks can make his Poems disrelished where they are but read and known." [32] Rymer could not have put it better. A consistent relativism would have held that the close relationship between Homer's art and the circumstances peculiar to his time seriously challenged the possibility of a *"Universal Ear."* But such consistency was rare.

# Chapter 5

# The Sources of Early

# Relativism

The principal ideas that contributed to the formation of relativist criticism in England warrant direct attention. At the outset there is a difficulty, for many of these ideas are themselves interrelated, some being logical extensions, some subdivisions, of others.

Still, the picture is far from chaotic. The important parts played by differences of language and the elusive notion of taste are separable from the welter of discussion. Avoiding the pitfalls of oversimplification and facile categorization of ideas, one may discern certain other recurrent relativist arguments. They have to do with race, nationality, or climate; religion; and the cultural, especially the literary, "climate." Yet another, the idea of progress, is reserved for separate treatment below, both because it is especially complex and because it comprehends many of the others.

Understandably enough, these concepts, or rather the ways in which they were conceived by some writers, were crude. By modern standards, for instance, the glib pronouncements about racial and national temperaments are shockingly "unscientific." But this is irrelevant to the problem we are dealing with here. What is significant is that critics in this early period pushed their speculations beyond mere vague statements about environmental differences, historical development, cultural contexts, and so forth. They were willing in many cases to specify what they considered to be the relevant differentiae. Obviously Athens was different from London. But which of the many divergences between the two bore upon literary production and evaluation? To this central question English critics before, during, and immediately following the Restoration offered answers. Not all of them can be called relativists, but the ideas they helped to make current lent themselves readily to the purposes of those who were.

Certain characteristics of a literary composition were sometimes traced to the climate in which the author had written it. In his "Preface to *Poems*" (1656) Abraham Cowley professed to find in the altered style of Ovid's work after his exile to Tomi on the Black Sea evidence of the effect of the cold. "The *cold* of the Countrey," he wrote, "had strucken through all his faculties, and benummed the very *feet* of his *Verses*." [1] Generally, though, the notion of climate as a determinant is allied or even identified with that of race or nationality, probably because racial or national traits were themselves regarded as effects of climate.[2] These traits accounted both for certain characteristics of a national literature and for the national taste, and consequently judgment. Neander, in

# The Sources of Early Relativism

Dryden's *An Essay of Dramatic Poesy* (1668), refers to the long, tedious declamations in French plays. Their actors, he remarks, "speak by the hour-glass, as our parsons do. . . . I deny not but this may suit well enough with the French; for as we, who are a more sullen people, come to be diverted at our plays, so they, who are of an airy and gay temper, come thither to make themselves more serious: and this I conceive to be one reason why comedy is more pleasing to us, and tragedies to them." [3]

St. Évremond traced to differences of national temperament the varied treatment of love and adventure in French and Spanish comedy. And of the relative irregularity of Spanish plays he writes: "As for *Regularity* and *Verisimilitude,* 'tis no wonder, we meet with 'em *less* among the *Spaniards,* than among the *French:* As all the *Spanish* galantry came from the *Moors,* there *still* remains in 't some *relish* of *Africa,* unknown to *other* nations, and too *extraordinary* to be *accomodated* to the exactness of *Rules.*" [4] English comedy he accounts for in the same way. He prefers the variety of its multiple action to the regularity and single action of the French. The English "humorous" characters, a factor in this variety, "being *ingeniously* form'd, are *carried* on too *far* according to *Frenchmen's* Opinions, as those of the *French* Theatre lye somewhat *heavy* on the *Stomach* of an *Englishman*. And the reason *hereof* is, perhaps, that the *English* think too much, and most commonly the *French* think *not enough.*" [5] The consequences of such views were inescapable. Although their implications for theories of literary evaluation were in part debatable and debated, one at least seemed beyond dispute. No poetic could be rigidly and literally established for all time—the main weapon in the relativist arsenal.

In this regard it should be kept in mind that even the most unyielding Aristotelians insisted that the *Poetics* was inductive, that its very cogency lay in the fact that its principles were derived *from* rather than imposed *upon* existing literature. This fact, easy to establish for Longinus as well, effectively countered the charge that the classical rules were arbitrary. Ultimately, however, it redounded against the absolutist position. For as critics came to believe that the structure of any literary genre was largely a product of national temperament and that temperamental differences among nations were apparent, an embarrassing question inevitably arose. To what extent was the form of Greek tragedy or epic, for example, merely an expression of something peculiarly Greek?

Roughly, a critic took one of three possible positions on this question, which, other things being equal, led him to absolutism of means and end, absolutism of end, or complete relativism. If he felt that peculiarities of national temperament were superficial, he could well enough maintain an extreme absolutism. If he considered such peculiarities significantly varying expressions of an essentially constant human nature, he embraced absolutism of end. If he saw them as radical differences, he argued for unqualified relativism. Not infrequently the same critic appears to have adopted each of these three positions at different times.

The problem engaged John Dennis. When in 1695 he

published a Pindaric ode on the death of Queen Mary, he felt the need for a definition of the ode, in particular of the type composed by Pindar. He wondered "how far it may be convenient to imitate him in our Age, and in our Language and Climate." Within the limitations imposed by the English language ("not capable of some of the most violent figures of *Pindar*") Dennis concluded that an Englishman might succeed in the Pindaric ode. "An *English* Writer may endeavour to imitate him in several of his greatest qualities, by the Genius of our Nation, which is bold and sublime, as Mr. *Waller* has observ'd." [6] Presumably a nation whose "genius" was not "bold and sublime" had better let the Pindaric ode alone.

The theory of race as a determinant of literary traits never quite disappeared during the years between the Restoration and the time when Taine included it as an element in his celebrated *Histoire*. In the period we are considering, however, more attention was paid to another "historical" factor: religion. In the seventeenth century particularly, when all things were put to the test of truth, it seemed imperative that the greatest of poetic genres should be based upon the only true religion: the epic would have to be Christian on penalty of being "false."

Moreover, as Davenant had argued, there were aesthetic as well as moral reasons for this. Hobbes agreed. "For as truth is the bound of Historical," he wrote, "so the Resemblance of truth is the utmost limit of Poeticall Liberty. In old time amongst the Heathen such strange fictions and Metamorphoses were not so remote from the Articles of their Faith as they are now from ours, and therefore were not so unpleasant." [7]

Abraham Cowley a few years later considered the poetic possibilities of the old mythology and concluded that the old poets had exhausted it. "Besides," he continued, "though those mad stories of the *Gods* and *Heroes* seem in themselves so ridiculous, yet they were then the *whole Body* (or rather *Chaos*) of the *Theologie* of those times. . . . There was no other *Religion,* and therefore *that* was better than *none at all.* But to us who have no need of them, to us who deride their *folly* and are wearied with their *impertinencies,* they ought to appear no better arguments for *Verse* then those of their worthy *Successors,* the *Knights Errant."* [8] This is perhaps as much the voice of the Royal Society as it is Cowley's. During this early period at least, much of the objection to the pagan epic was part of the more general objection to all literary "vanities"; in the same spirit Bishop Sprat was soon to inveigh against stylistic "impertinencies" in prose.

Probably because the Christian epic was discussed as a separate issue in France by Boileau and others, Dryden addresses himself to it three decades later. The French critics had in the meantime complicated the question by expressing doubt that the heroic and the Christian spirits were reconcilable. Modern epic poets, according to this reasoning, were handicapped by a religion whose stress on patience and humility ill sorted with the heroic themes of action, war, and boundless

75

ambition. True, Dryden conceded, but since great persons in public places may, consistent with Christian principle, show "prudence, counsel, active fortitude, coercive power, awful command," and the like, he concluded "that an Epic Poem . . . may be as well written now, as it was of old by the heathens; provided the poet be endued with the same talents. . . ." [9] (His exception as to language, "that only inferiority," we have already examined.)

Objection to a Christian epic was expressed in England as well as in France. Dryden may well have been thinking of Sir William Temple. Among other reasons why modern poetry was absolutely inferior to the ancient, Temple maintained that Christian themes were not so well adapted to fiction as were those of the false religions. Their effect, he felt, had been "rather to debase Religion than to heighten Poetry." [10] The whole controversy presented the would-be epic poet with a dilemma forcing a choice between doing violence to his aesthetics or his piety—or those of his critics and readers. To use Christian themes was a sacrilege; to use pagan was poetically ineffective.[11]

One of these epic poets, Sir Richard Blackmore, took care to defend his own practice against the strictures of Temple and others. *"My Opinion* has always differ'd from these Gentlemen's; I believe a *Christian Poet* has as great advantages as the *Pagan* had, and that our *Theology* may enter into an Epick Poem and *raise* the Subject without being it self *debas'd."* [12] Twenty years later he reiterates this view, scoffing at scruples against the use of Christian "machinery." In fact, to use pagan "machines," he holds, is absurd. ". . . Epick Poetry is indeed the Theology of the Country where the Poet lives . . . a sort of Confession of the Publick Faith there establish'd. . . ." [13]

Blackmore's position here is of course relativist. But it is also in keeping with his predominantly moralistic criteria. The poet, above all the epic poet, must edify if nothing else. Baldly put, this meant preaching Christian principles in Christian times. Dennis, though he agreed with Blackmore in the matter of Christian poetry, based his argument less on moral than on aesthetic, and pragmatic, considerations. Moreover, he made a far more searching analysis of the place of religion in poetry. He lists nine rules for its proper treatment, the second of which provides that the poet must use the "reigning" faith in order that the reader may be more impressed. "And this Rule may acquaint us with one of the Reasons why all who have translated *Homer* and *Virgil,* have succeeded so very indifferently." [14] Unlike Blackmore, Dennis was troubled not so much with the "falsity" of the pagan epic as with the effect of that "falsity": the failure of the poem to induce pleasurable admiration in the reader. On the same grounds he contrasted, favorably to himself, his own use of epic "machines" in *The Battle of Ramillia* with Boileau's in his fourth *Epistle.* "For my Machines are Christian whereas his are Pagan, and consequently can raise no great Emotion in the Minds of the Readers, because they are incredible, according to one of his own Verses.—*L'esprit n'est point emu de ce qu'il ne croit pas.*" [15]

Dennis, however, less a slave to his own theories than

# The Sources of Early Relativism

has sometimes been supposed, was honest and intelligent enough to see difficulties. He maintained constantly his position that the greatest poetic forms, including of course the epic, were essentially religious and therefore, in modern Europe, Christian. But examination of the details of epic structure suggested the need for some modification of his own general principle. Given his abiding interest in the problem, his study of Milton's great exemplum was inevitable. And though Dennis need yield to no man in his admiration of *Paradise Lost,* it did not blind him to

> one Unhappiness that attends our modern Poetry: For tho' the Machines with which the Christian Religion supplies us, must be allow'd to be greater, more wonderful, and more terrible, than any which the Pagan Religion affords us, they are less delightful: For that which comes nearest to humane Nature, must in Poetry be most delightful to it; but the Gods and Goddesses of the *Grecian* and *Roman* Poetry, being feign'd to have manifest Bodies, and apparent humane Shapes, and the agreeable Distinction of Sexes, come incomparably nearer to humane Nature, than the Machines of the Christian Poetry, and are therefore more delightful to it. . . .

This is an interesting admission from one who had argued for the potential absolute superiority (*actual* in Milton) of modern epic poetry over ancient on the ground that Christianity was more moving because truer and thus more sublime. Probably Dennis felt what many Milton readers have felt since, an imperfect sympathy with completely nonhuman characters. In fact his immediate purpose is to defend Milton against the charge of confounding "Body and Mind, Spirit and Matter," in his angels.[16] But this more or less technical difficulty raises again a critical problem transcending the immediate question of Milton's achievement. If supernatural machinery is a formal element essential to the epic as a genre, may works in that genre not be limited to cultures whose religions are anthropomorphic and polytheistic? Whether consciously or not, critics like Dryden, Temple, and Dennis were really investigating one of the most challenging conclusions of the relativist aesthetic: that genres themselves, the fundamental forms of literary expression, die out. This matter is not settled by the allegation (which may be true) that the divine machinery is not an element essential to the epic structure. For that merely leads back to the initial problem: the definition of "epic."

Of the many factors that comprise the complex and elusive concept variously denominated the cultural "climate," the historical setting, or the intellectual matrix of a literary work, the most immediate, as Professor René Wellek has pointed out,[17] is the literary tradition itself. In the subject matter and the form of their writing authors are probably more influenced by the practice of their fellows than by any other factor. Their work is affected not only by the cast of contemporary writing but also by the kind of writing produced in the generation just past. What may be called the literary "climate" has been regarded by relativist critics as necessarily conditioning critical appraisal.

79

# The Sources of Early Relativism

This consideration, in fact, underlies the protest against questions like "Is Pope a better poet than Keats?" The familiar retort that they are not subject to evaluative comparison, that they did "different things," is at base a relativist answer. It implies that as early eighteenth and early nineteenth century English poetic production were governed by divergent literary modes, so they must be judged by separate critical standards. In this regard the relativist position appears to best advantage when, let us say, it is urged that to condemn Wordsworth for not doing what Pope had done is to condemn him for not doing the impossible. Such criticism is therefore unfair if not meaningless. But all of this depends on another notion: that the peculiar excellence of one literary age cannot be repeated in the following, that one can speak of the "exhaustion" of a literary manner.

Cowley defended his choice of a Biblical topic for his *Davideis* by attacking the "lying" fables of the Ancients. But he offered the further excuse that the classical themes were worn out anyway. "I do not at all wonder," he observes, "that the old Poets made some rich crops out of these grounds; the heart of the *Soil* was not then wrought out with continual *Tillage*. But what can we expect now, who come a *Gleaning,* not after the first *Reapers* but after the very *Beggars?*" [18] This is somewhat crude; but clearly Cowley is asking not to be censured for failing to do what could no longer be done.

Dryden probes more deeply into the problem as part of his defense of rhymed tragedy in the *Essay of Dramatic Poesy*. He admits that he and his contemporaries could never equal the work of Shakespeare, Beaumont, and Jonson. But, he adds, "they could never equal themselves, were they to rise and write again. We acknowledge them our fathers in wit; but they have ruined their estates themselves, before they came to their children's hands. . . . All comes sullied or wasted to us: and were they to entertain this age, they could not make so plenteous treatments out of such decayed fortunes." [19]

What is of special interest here is the phrase "they could never equal themselves." For what Dryden clearly means is that the literary tradition imposes limitations on even the greatest talents.[20] Once this is granted, it becomes incumbent upon the critic never to pass judgment on a writer in disregard of his literary environment. As for the writer, he must choose "either not to write at all, or to attempt some other way." Dryden's conclusion was that only writing rhymed verse remained unexploited for the Restoration tragedians. Judged in this light, they must be given a higher rating, for "our age is arrived to a perfection in it, which they [the Elizabethans] never knew." [21]

To translate such a critical method into responsible practice required a greater knowledge of literary history, of the concept of periods and movements, than Dryden's age could command. Yet its recognition probably tempered if it did not entirely prevent a certain amount of inconsiderate judicial pronouncement. When Dryden himself objected to Jonson's "clenches," Gerard Langbaine suggested the possibility that " 'twas his Compliance with the Age that induc'd him to this way of writing, it being then, as Mr. *Dryden* observes, the Mode of Wit, the Vice of the Age, and not Ben *Johnson's*. . . ." [22] It led also to an enrichment of the whole study of literature, to a more mature understanding of the intricacies of the critical function broadly conceived. The earliest and least defensible absolutism had naïvely thought of the creative act as one of unfettered will. Given something called genius and something else called art, the poet was free to fashion as he would. On the surface, this seems to glorify the creative artist; ultimately, it cheapens him. Only when they have recognized that the artist is a man among men, that his achievement is effected within limitations and against obstacles, do critics begin truly to appreciate as well as to comprehend him. For then it becomes apparent that artistic virtue is not cloistered.

This recognition was enriching too in its concept of the product, as distinct from the producer, by suggesting that any work, especially great work, was the result of a coincidence of forces of which the individual creative gift was only one. Thus Dennis came to conclude that there were "Three Things that contribute to the Perfection of Poetry; so that in any Age or Country, at whatever Juncture Religion and Language, and Poetical Art, are in greatest Force together, at that very Juncture the Poetry of that Country is at its Heighth. And this is the Reason why Tragedy, which is a Poem of the Growth of *Attica,* was at its Heighth in the Time of *Sophocles,* because then the Language was in Perfection; the Art of Poetry, and particularly of Tragedy, had been extremely cultivated, and Religion as yet had Power enough o'er the Mind of Men to inforce the Passions." [23]

For the moment we are concerned with only the third of Dennis' factors, "Poetical Art," an element of the literary "climate." It is frequently maintained that *Lycidas* and *Adonais* owe part of their excellence to the established tradition of the pastoral elegy. Milton and Shelley had a form ready at hand upon which they wrought happy variations. At a commendably early date Dennis intimated much the same thing of Sophocles' plays.

This does not necessarily lessen the praise due the writer. It asks only—what the relativist always asks—that the critic determine first the nature of what he means to judge in order properly to adjust his criterion. It implies too that the nature of the object can best be determined by seeing it as a resultant of several forces, among them the literary tradition obtaining at the time and place of composition. The passages quoted from Cowley and Dryden suggest that sometimes the literary conditions are inhibitive, that the artist has relatively little freedom. That from Dennis shows that it may also liberate and enhance the individual talent. In his purely evaluative function the critic can do justice in the first case by mitigating his severity, by shortening the "scale"; in the second he may do more than justice by applying other than the most rigorous standards.[24] In neither case would an absolute measurement be valid, since what would fit the one would be inapplicable to the other.

This, in the opinion of some writers, was Rymer's prime critical sin (though here it included more than the literary "climate"). In his *Short View,* Charles Gildon observed, Rymer had failed to distinguish between the faults of Shakespeare and those of his age. Gildon mentions three conditions prevalent in Shakespeare's time to account for many things in *Othello* for which Rymer had blamed the dramatist himself: the taste of the audience for tragicomedy; the lack of financial support for the stage similar to that enjoyed by the Greeks; and the need to write to the talent of the actors.[25] However debatable may be Gildon's choice of governing conditions, his argument that allowing for them would have spared Shakespeare at least the more violent Rymerian epithets shows how historical analysis and relativist appraisal may be related.

Absolutism of the dogmatic variety could not stand in the face of arguments of this sort. As attention to environmental factors increased, the position became gradually untenable. Still, it was not to be entirely overcome by squabbles over the merits of Shakespeare and Spenser, based as it was on the great classics. The Drydens and Gildons, however, had unknown allies, scholars and antiquaries who were beginning to apply to the classics themselves this same environmental approach and to discover the dependence of their content and form upon contemporary circumstances of life and art. The work of Richard Bentley, notably his *Dissertation on the Letters of Phalaris* (1697), is an instance. Unfortunately, the social gap between university and coffee house prevented as much exchange of ideas between scholar and poet-critic as might otherwise have been.

# The Sources of Early Relativism

Sometimes, though, the two pursuits met in one man. Samuel Wesley, who wrote an epic with Christ as the hero, incorporated into his "Essay on Heroic Poetry" ideas gathered from his studies in Mediterranean languages and literatures. He explains Homer's mythology historically and causally, he derives Greek and Latin from ancient Phoenician, and he discovers a historical reason for the fictitious epic hero. Bossu had made this last point an absolute rule; Wesley's relativism shows itself when he argues, against Bossu, that Homer's use of mythical heroes for his epics was an accident of the times, all learning then being mythological. Now, he concludes, an epic poet may perfectly well use a historical figure as hero.[26]

What was probably the first attempt at an extended application of this method to classical literature did not appear until 1735, when Thomas Blackwell published *An Enquiry into the Life and Writings of Homer*. His book tells a detailed, perhaps too ingenious, story of Homer's education and travels, including an account of the Egyptian, Phoenician, and other sources of the Greek religion and mythology. His findings convinced him that Homer's works were something less than miracles of individual genius. "Such Reflections as these," he writes, "have sometimes led me to think, that HOMER's *Art* was not so great and refined, as we commonly suppose it to have been: That his *Good Fortune* was far superiour to his *Skill;* since he needed but represent things both in his own and other Countries, *almost as he heard them talked of.*" Homer, it seems, could hardly help producing great work.

85

# The Sources of Early Relativism

"Thus, We have run over *Homer's* Advantages from Nature and Education: We have surveyed the *Climate* where he was born: We have considered the *Manners* of his Country, its *Language* and *Religion;* and have found from the Nature of things, and their constant Effects, that they were *all* in the happiest temper for Description and Poesy." [27]

Despite the credit given Blackwell for his contribution to the development of criticism, it must be said that the seventeenth century critics had already conceived of and defended the method he used. Minus the doubtful documentation, Dennis a generation earlier took much the same view of Sophocles as Blackwell here does of Homer.[28]

One of the most arresting and surely the most enduring of the relativist arguments growing out of these notions was the doctrine of genre decay. Might a genre itself, rather than merely certain of its structural details, have depended entirely on conditions racial, religious, economic, political, linguistic, no longer obtaining? "In every form of artistic production," Sir Leslie Stephen declared,

> in painting and architecture, for example, schools arise; each of which seems to embody some kind of principle, and develops and afterwards decays, according to some mysterious law. It may resemble the animal species which is, somehow or other, developed and then stamped out of existence by the growth of a form more appropriate to the new order. The epic poem, shall we say? is like the 'monstrous efts,' as Tennyson unkindly called them, which were

86

no doubt very estimable creatures in their day, but have somehow been unable to adapt themselves to recent geological epochs.[29]

Still engaging critical attention, the question is asked mostly with respect to tragedy and the epic, but not exclusively. Dennis' remarks about the Pindaric ode imply that in certain racial and linguistic conditions that form would be impossible. Actually, more than one current of seventeenth century thought led up to the problem. The "Ancients"–"Moderns" quarrel, the earlier belief in nature's decay, and the later idea of progress variously bear upon it. The last in particular. For progress implies at least the possibility of regress; if one could trace the development, *ab origine,* of a literary form (as many were now doing), one could surely envision its decline and extinction.

In general Dryden resisted the idea, though he did of course insist that each age had to adapt a genre to its own "genius." But it troubled him, and he had to grant that it might be true. "But suppose that Homer and Virgil were the only of their species, and that Nature was so much worn out in producing them, that she is never able to bear the like again, yet the example only holds in Heroic Poetry: in Tragedy and Satire, I offer myself to maintain against some of our modern critics, that this age and the last, particularly in England, have excelled the ancients in both those kinds. . . ."[30] In this instance Dryden does not consider the phenomenon causally, except in terms of the vague and already exploded notion of nature's decay.

# The Sources of Early Relativism

Two years later, however, William Wotton did so in his *Reflections upon Ancient and Modern Learning* (1694). In his third chapter he considers oratory and poetry as they existed in three periods: the Greek, the Roman, and the modern. The quality of what was produced in these two branches of literature, Wotton argues, is owing neither to natural gifts nor to "Art" (i.e. study), but to prevalent linguistic and political conditions. "That these Accidents, and not a particular Force of Genius, raised the *Grecian* Poesie and Oratory, will further appear, if we reflect upon the History of the Rise and Increase of both those Arts amongst the *Romans*." Because of the peculiar suitability of their language to prosody, the Greeks had an advantage over the Romans in poetry, except for "Philosophical and Epical Poems." Latin's "Majestick Gravity" made possible the achievements of Virgil and Lucretius in these kinds. As for the modern languages, Italian, French, and English, their varying accentuation determines their relative suitability to "some sorts of Poems." [31]

Wotton doubts that the modern languages would ever have produced the epic. Answering Temple, who had insisted on the superior genius of the Ancients, he presses his point: "though a very great deal is to be given to the Genius and Judgment of the Poet, which are both absolutely necessary to make a good Poem, what Tongue soever the Poet writes in, yet the Language it self has so great an Influence, that if *Homer* and *Virgil* had been *Polanders* or *High-Dutch-Men,* they would never in all probability have thought it worth their while to attempt

88

the Writing of Heroick Poems. . . ." [32] This statement is significant on two counts: it proposes that language may determine not alone the style of a genre but the very possibility of that genre's existence; [33] moreover, it conceives of art forms not as products of unfettered individual inventiveness but of forces beyond human control. Accepted as premises, these in turn point inevitably to the doctrine of genre decay.

Similarly, Wotton founds oratory upon political circumstances. Eloquence is a plant that flourishes only in the soil of political freedom.

> When Orators are no longer Constituent Parts of a Government, or, at least, when Eloquence is not an almost certain Step to arrive at the chiefest Honours in a State, the Necessity of the Art of Speaking is in a great measure taken off; and as the Authority of Orators lessens, which it will insensibly do as Tyranny and Absolute Power prevail, their Art will dwindle into Declamation, and an Affectation of Sentences and Forms of Wit. . . . It is Liberty alone which inspires Men with Lofty Thoughts, and elevates their Souls to a higher Pitch than Rules of Art can direct. [34]

This notion was not original with Wotton or even with his century. Longinus himself refers in the final chapter of *On the Sublime* to the view that no slave ever becomes an orator. But in Wotton's day, when the nature of literature was being subjected to fresh and penetrating examination, it took on new cogency.

John Dennis' early recognition of the relationship between literary form and environment made it almost inevitable that he should declare himself on the question.

89

His most interesting pronouncement came after years devoted to the study of poetic problems, especially in tragedy and the epic. Poetry, he concluded, is dependent on other branches of learning—mathematics, physics, metaphysics, and so forth. The "explosion" of any of these sciences would thus affect the value of the poetry dependent on them. More than that, it could put an end to further production of work in a whole genre. "The poem that has done most Honour to England," he writes of *Paradise Lost*, "is Three Fourths of it metaphysicks; which part of learning if we should wholly explode . . . I am afraid we must banish machines from Poetry, and soe Turn Heroick Poetry quite out of the world." [35]

Like many of the other concepts that lent support to relativist critical appraisal, this one influenced the study of literature in other directions. It contributed, doubtless, to the decreasing concern with genres, with the Renaissance preoccupation with classifying literature in general and poetry in particular into types. For once they are seen as relative rather than absolute, the study of the genres themselves and the distinctions between them seem less important. Such modern academic approaches to literature as those which trace the origin of the novel to socio-economic changes and study its development in terms of middle-class culture are a familiar product of this environmentalism.

The list of those who in some form or other gave expression to ideas supporting relativism during the earlier neoclassical period clearly includes many illustrious names. Some who contributed most to the historical and environmental concept moved from a tentative relativism to a final absolutism. Dennis was one of these. Others were simply inconsistent. The fact remains that notions of race, language, religion, and literary or cultural "climate" ultimately closed the dead-end road of critical dogmatism. They opened not one but many new approaches, all of which have enriched the study of literature. Among them was one which envisioned the possibility and desirability of relativist critical criteria.

# Chapter 6

# The Idea of Progress

The rise of relativist literary criticism is not entirely explained by the concepts race, religion, language, and cultural setting. An idea of more far-reaching consequences transcending these concepts and to some extent produced by them—the doctrine of progress—provided an intellectual atmosphere favorable to the genesis of new theories in literature, as in other fields of thought. Apart from this context, the origin of relativism is imperfectly understood, and its failure to achieve a complete and lasting victory over absolutism cannot be understood at all. For by a kind of irony not uncommon in intellectual history, the idea which did most to promote early relativism was the same which ultimately prevented its triumph. An intelligible analysis of this ideational complex requires a review of the development of the doctrine of progress stressing its special bearings on our subject.

The notion of progress, a more or less consciously held belief that human knowledge and institutions partake of a gradual ameliorative development through time, is comparatively modern. As J. B. Bury has shown in his valu-

# The Idea of Progress

able book, "the intellectual climates of classical antiquity and the ensuing ages were not propitious to the birth of the doctrine of Progress. It is not till the sixteenth century that the obstacles to its appearance definitely begin to be transcended and a favourable atmosphere to be gradually prepared." [1]

Notable among these obstacles was an opposite belief that had long dominated men's minds: the principle of nature's decay. All of nature, including man himself, it was thought, had been steadily deteriorating since the Creation.[2] Man's intellectual and moral powers, the earth's fertility, even the size of trees, were all thought to be declining. The pagan myths of a golden age and the Hebrew myth of a garden of Eden doubtless lay behind this depressing notion. Whatever its source, it profoundly affected Renaissance attitudes toward fresh human endeavor, especially in science and literature. "Probably no single factor," R. F. Jones writes, "was so responsible for the feeling of modern inferiority as the belief that all nature was decaying in its old age. It lay, indeed, at the bottom of most manifestations of the worship of antiquity, though frequently not finding expression in words." [3]

Not until this pessimism had been dissipated could the progress idea take hold. The notion of decay did not die easily. In 1622 Henry Peacham's *The Compleat Gentleman* warned against the habit of "imagining nature hath heretofore extracted her quintessence and left vs the dregges. . . ." Yet ten years later Henry Reynolds opened his *Mythomystes* with the remark that the world is grown

93

decrepit and sick.[4] Its denial followed two courses of reasoning, both consistent with a faith in progress. Some, following Bacon's *Antiquitas seculi iuventus mundi,* declared that the passage of years increased man's potentialities by adding to the sum of his knowledge, that the race matured rather than aged. This in itself is a crude form of "progressism." Others were content only to refute the view that nature was subject to alteration in any of her processes, maintaining the principle of the invariability of natural law. Though less sanguine on the surface, this position was the more fruitful in preparing the way for the doctrine of progress. For, among other things, it supplied the logical assumption necessary for scientific discovery.

The final victory of the idea of progress over that of decay appears to have resulted from the celebrated Battle of the Books. The "Moderns," by asserting the permanence of nature's powers, succeeded at last in bringing the degeneration theory into disrepute. During most of the seventeenth century, the many disputes over the relative merits of classical and modern authors regularly reduced themselves to the issue of progression versus retrogression. In France, as late as 1688, Fontenelle, whose *Digression sur les Anciens et les Modernes* was perhaps the greatest single contribution to the "Modern" cause, devoted much of his pamphlet to proving that man's nature remains constant, that the Moderns are not lesser men than the Ancients, and that the dissimilarities between them are merely circumstantial. Once this point was established, it was easy to make a convincing case for the indefinite progress not of human nature but of human knowledge. Since later generations had always the advantage of what had been discovered before, their advance in knowledge was almost inevitable; moreover, it was independent of individual ability.[5]

From this theory, to be sure, there was non-degenerationist dissent too. For the belief in progress Sir William Temple substituted his well known theory of cultural cycles. "Science and Arts," he wrote, "have run their circles, and had their periods in the several Parts of the World." Lumped indiscriminately together, philosophy, the sciences, and the arts are subject to recurrent rounds of growth and decay. Espousing the cause of the "Ancients," Temple believed that the period from pagan times to his own represented the decay part of the current cycle. In philosophy not even Descartes and Hobbes, whom he considers the only possible claimants, had "eclipsed the Lustre of *Plato, Aristotle, Epicurus,* or others of the Ancients." In grammar, rhetoric, and poetry no modern except Fontenelle (whose poems belie his claim) had dared to think his work equal to the classics. Finally, with a blind assurance that played directly into the hands of his "Modern" opponents, Temple finds nothing new in astronomy except the Copernican system, nor in *"Physick"* except *"Hervy's* Circulation of the blood." And, he avers, it is even a matter of dispute whether these are new or "derived from old Fountains." [6]

Although today Temple's arguments are recalled principally as part of a literary controversy, from the point of view of the history of ideas they are most significant as a kind of "minority report" on the question of progress. Accurately defined, his position is rather a modification than an outright denial of progressism. Its acceptance did not necessarily commit one to the "Ancient" side, much less to critical absolutism.[7]

Meanwhile, on both sides of the English channel, the visible achievements of mathematicians and natural scientists had provided such telling force to the doctrine of progress that by the late seventeenth century it was embraced by the greater part of the educated public. Their persuasion was uncritical by modern standards, especially in one particular. Because the distinction we now make between arts and sciences was generally overlooked, critics, sometimes unconsciously, drew between the two a hasty and unwarranted analogy by which artistic attainment was considered chronologically cumulative.[8]

Wotton is a notable exception. Refuting Perrault's thesis that modern poets and orators were superior to the ancient, he pointed to the "wide Difference between an Art that, having no Antecedent Foundation in Nature, owes its first Original to some particular Invention, and all its future Improvements to Superstructures raised by other Men upon that first Ground-work; and between Passions of the Mind that are Congenial with our Natures, where Conversation will polish them, even without previous Intentions of doing so, and where the Experiences of a few Ages, if assisted by Books that may preserve particular Cases, will carry them to as great an Heighth as the Things themselves are capable of." Wotton deserves the general commendation he has since received for his clear-sightedness in this matter. Of most enduring validity perhaps is his exposure of the critical absurdities to which the mere assumption of indefinite aesthetic progress leads. Perrault, he observes, concluded that Cicero was a better orator than Demosthenes because he had the advantage of two hundred years further improvement of the art. By this logic, "the Gentlemen of the Academy must out-do *Tully* for the same Reasons." Far from supporting a theory of unbroken progress, Wotton continues, literary history shows that there may be retrogression: a Seneca and a younger Pliny followed a Cicero.[9]

It is against this background of conception and misconception that we must read the frequent unfavorable comparisons of contemporary achievement in the arts to that in other fields. Typical is a passage quoted by Sir Thomas Pope Blount from John Norris' "Preface to his Collection of Miscellanies": "It may (says Norris) appear strange indeed, that in such a *Refining* Age as this, wherein all things seem ready to receive their *last Turn* and *finishing Stroke,* Poetry should be the only thing, that remains unimprov'd." [10] Writing in the last decade of the century, Blount might well have cited many similar expressions of puzzlement or complaint. Occasionally, as here, the discrepancy is regarded simply as an unaccountable phenomenon; in some instances the poets are charged with remissness. Most often, however, critics more cheerfully conclude that "such a *Refining* Age" argues the likelihood of poetry's soon following suit. A few, of

97

course, had always had an implicit faith in the independent advancement of poetry; for these the fact of scientific progress merely made their argument apply a fortiori. Common to all was a belief in literary progress.

The doctrine of literary imitation, in essence both antirelativist and antiprogressive, was bound to be challenged after the appearance of Bacon's *Advancement of Learning*. Ben Jonson, concluding a discussion of good and bad styles with a direct reference to Bacon's three "distempers of learning," expressed his impatience with a slavish attitude toward the past in literary matters. "Nothing is more ridiculous," he wrote, "then to make an Author a *Dictator,* as the schooles have done *Aristotle.* . . . Let *Aristotle* and others have their dues; but if wee can make farther Discoveries of truth and fitnesse then they, why are we envied?" [11] Only with the strictest reservations could Jonson be called a "Modern." He has no faith in inevitable progress and was certainly far from thinking everything the classical writers had done was inferior, and therefore had been or could be better done by moderns. His plea is only for the potential of literary progress and against a commitment to imitation that would stifle that potential.

This kind of enlightened classicism is apparent later in Sir William Davenant, who regarded imitation as a mixed blessing. Homer is useful to the epic poet "as Seamarks are chiefly useful to Coasters, and serve not those who have the ambition of Discoverers, that love to sail in untry'd Seas, so he hath rather prov'd a Guide for those whose satisfy'd Wit will not venture beyond the track of others, then to them who affect a new and remote way of thinking, who esteem it a deficiency and meaness of minde to stay and depend upon the authority of example." Imitation, he admitted, was a check upon error, but, "Such limits to the progress of every thing, even of worthiness as well as defect, doth Imitation give; for whilst we imitate others, we can no more excel them, then he that sailes by others Mapps can make a new discovery. . . ."

Like Jonson, Davenant used the hope of artistic development as the basis for a declaration of artistic freedom. And even this is done less defiantly than defensively. "If I be accus'd of Innovation," he writes, "or to have transgressed against the method of the Ancients, I shall think my self secure in beleeving that a Poet, who hath wrought with his own instruments at a new design, is no more answerable for disobedience to his Predecessors, then *Law-makers* are liable to those old Laws which themselves have repealed." [12]

Actually, it would be at least inaccurate to cite such passages as these in support of the theory of aesthetic progress. True, Davenant did believe he could produce a better epic than Homer's or Virgil's; but that he ascribed to a propitious historical "accident"—the prevalence of Christianity—not to an assumed improvement in the art by knowledge accumulated through time. Jonson envisioned "farther," not *better,* "Discoveries of truth"; Davenant's "excel them," appearing in the context of "new and remote way" and "new design," should perhaps be understood as an addition of *other* rather than a substitution of *better*. These critics contemplated development and innovation, not amelioration that necessarily discredited past achievement.

Critically, such views strongly suggested some kind of relativism, since a dynamic art could scarcely be judged by fixed criteria. But the problem was soon to be complicated. For men began to notice that modern scientific accomplishment was not merely a development from but an improvement upon the ancient. Furthermore, this improvement involved a rejection of the old way in many cases, since it was logical to substitute better for worse, if not indeed truth for error. It was this concept of progress which, largely under the influence of scientific achievement, came to predominate. As long as its application to literature was limited to the view that literary production must improve in time, relativist critical theory was defensible. It could be argued that the work of each age was best judged by its own measure: Aristotle's *Poetics* remained a useful guide to Greek though not to modern poetry. This position was closely allied to and consistent with environmental relativism.

There was, however, another and perhaps more logical argument. If poetry, like physics and mathematics, improves, then surely critical theory, being derived from it, must improve too. The modern critic, endowed with a refined instrument, must therefore be the best judge of any literary work past or present. Modern literary theory, in other words, could replace ancient aesthetic "error" with new aesthetic "truth." The analogy with scientific progress thus led to a new critical absolutism.[13] Along with the prevailing "mathematicism" examined above, this helps to explain too why critics like Dennis, whose early writings contained strong relativist tendencies, were later to propound absolutist theories.

In his letter to Harrington in defense of the modern poets, Charles Gildon declares that the poetry of ancient Greece "still maintains its Share of Glory and Esteem, whilst her Philosophy is now exploded by the Universal Reason of Mankind." The old poets, he concedes, will be great "as long as they are understood," but Aristotle the philosopher "is now shrunk" to the status of critic or grammarian.[14] Elsewhere he questions accepting the authority of the Greeks in poetry when they "had not the advantage of us in *Physics,* or any other part of Philosophy. . . . Since the time of *Des Cartes,* when the Dictates of *Greece* began to be laid aside, what a Progress has been made in the discovery of Nature? and what Absurdities laid open in the School Precepts, and Terms of *Aristotle.*" Why, he asks, when they have been bested in the most difficult sciences, is such deference paid to their humanistic learning? [15]

Defending the use of love themes in modern tragedy, he abandons the historical relativism, by which he has just accounted for their absence from the Greek stage, for the absolutist thesis that such motifs ought to be employed in all tragedy. This, he admits, contradicts Greek practice and Aristotelian theory. "But since the *Ipse dixit* has been so long laid aside in Philosophy, as an enemy to our Enquiries into Nature, I can see no reason why it shou'd be of so much greater force in Poetry; since 'tis perhaps almost as prejudicial to our imitation of Nature in *This,* as to our discovery of it in the Other." This is an example, though not a perfect one, of incipient relativism being turned into absolutism by the assumption that literary theory progresses like scientific theory. It is imperfect because Gildon does admit ancient authority if it passes the test of "good sense and Nature," [16] suggesting that *some* of the ancient lore might be valid.

Nonetheless, the fact of modern invalidation of ancient science suggested strongly to him that ancient literature too was inferior and the literary theory based upon it consequently discredited. It was, moreover, a suggestion counter to the historical relativism he seems most concerned to establish. Like other critics in revolt against dogmatic absolutism, Gildon seized upon weapons highly effective against the "Ancients" but ultimately irreconcilable as bases for any positive theory of judgment: the principle of environmental contexts and the doctrine of artistic progress (in the sense of steady improvement). The first seemed to indicate relativism whereas the second would scarcely admit it.[17] For the new scientific theories were absolute.

They were, that is, for the most part. A curious exception to this rule allowed Gildon to combine the science analogy with environmentalism in support of a relativist aesthetic. Medical theory was regarded by some as historically variable. Granting the Ancients credit for inventing arts and sciences, Gildon "cannot without contradicting [his] own Reason, allow them the Perfecters of 'em so far that they must be our uncontroverted Patterns and Standards: For our Physicians have found the Prescripts of *Hippocrates* very Defective: And as in Physic, so in Poetry, there must be a regard had to the Clime, Nature, and Customs of the People; for the Habits of the Mind as well as those of the Body, are influenc'd by them; and Love with the other Passions vary in their *Effects* as well as *Causes,* according to each Country and Age. . . ." Interesting and ingenious as this analogy is, it is worth noting that Gildon does not apply it to the work at hand. He defends the love poems of Cowley and Waller in absolutist terms. Their occasions, he maintains, are as natural and universally understandable as those of Ovid and Catullus.[18]

Writing on the epic, Sir Richard Blackmore reminds his readers of the overthrow of Aristotelian authority in "philosophy," but not in poetry. He is puzzled as to why the proponents of "the free Exercise of Reason" have made this exception. "They had as great Reason to have proceeded to the Examination of his Rules in the Art of Poetry. . . . But I know not how it came to pass, his Notions and Precepts in this Art have still remain'd unquestion'd and untry'd. The modern Criticks, contemning the Examples of the Philosophers, have still proceeded in the old beaten Track, of believing and admiring whatever *Aristotle* advances on the Subjects, where the Muses are concern'd." By the time he wrote this, Blackmore's allegation against modern criticism was no longer justified, but his attitude warrants examination nonetheless. It assumes the possibility of aesthetic progress and attributes its supposed absence to the critics' failure to apply to their subject the method fruitfully employed by philosophers and scientists ("the free Exercise of Reason"). This failure, which Blackmore can only ascribe to a foolish reverence for ipse dixit, has hampered poetry's natural tendency to progress. Aristotle was, of course, "A great Genius," but Blackmore will "no more submit to him as a Law-giver of the Poets, than of the Philosophers. . . . And if Men, from a generous Principle of Liberty, would renounce the unjust, the prevailing Power of Authority, and claim their natural Right of entring into the Reason of Things, and judging for themselves, it is highly probable that the Art of Poetry might be carry'd on to greater Degrees of Perfection, and be improv'd, as Philosophy has been." Such attacks were dear to the hearts of the relativists, since, as Blackmore added, adoption of the method he urged meant that epic poets would no longer be judged by the standards of the *Iliad* and the *Aeneid*.[19]

Yet, this essay points up the falsity of equating the "revolt against the classical rules" with relativism. For Blackmore, consistent with his notion of poetic progress, substituted for the standard of the classical epic not a *relative* standard but "the Nature and Constitution of that kind of Poetry." No standard could be more absolute. Blackmore displays no tolerance for other "modes." He explains the presence of "Knight-Errantry, Sorcery, and incredible Atchievements" in Ariosto and Spenser by tracing the romance tradition from Heliodorus through the Provençal to the Renaissance writers. But he condemns it as "the general Infection of the Times," as an art which violated probability, an "essential Rule of Poetry." The older English poets too are not merely different but inferior. It is not a question of varying standards of taste. "It is a sordid Disposition of Mind," he writes in the section of his essay entitled "Of the Choice of Words," "that makes any Men prefer their rustick and offensive Stile, before those pure and beautiful Forms of Speech which our Tongue abounds with. . . ." And this proposed substitution of a new set of absolute rules in place of the old is predicated on the belief in aesthetic progress. Universality and antiquity have much weight "but since they have often been produc'd to support manifest Errors in Philosophy as well as in Religion, and have therefore been often rejected, why should they be regarded as infallible in Poetry?" [20] In every field of human endeavor the Ancients had done much, but, after all, modern man had in the method of "Reason" the key to the portal of Truth.

Environmentalism and the doctrine of progress were joined in another way to produce a somewhat less naïve theory of literary advancement. An early translator of St. Évremond takes the position that the Ancients excelled the Moderns in that ability to describe nature and the human passions which makes great literature. But since a knowledge of many details—"Decorum, Contrivance,

Oeconomy, etc"—is necessary to such description, Moderns have the advantage in discovering "Rules and Precepts that can never be found out but by a long train of Experience and Reflection. . . ." [21] This reasoning is more than and different from the rather shallow modernism Blackmore was to exhibit years later. It comprehends aesthetic progress as a function of the general increase of nonaesthetic knowledge, not as an autonomous phenomenon: literature and literary theory, as resultants of prevalent institutions, "progress" because those institutions "progress." The relationship of literary progress to scientific and philosophic progress is thus one not of simple analogy but of cause and effect.

"It must be acknowledg'd," wrote St. Évremond himself, "that *Aristotle's* ART of POETRY is an excellent Piece of Work: But however there's nothing so perfect in it, as to be the standing Rule of all Nations, and all Ages. *Descartes* and *Gassendi* have found out Truths, that were unknown to *Aristotle. Corneille* has discover'd Beauties for the Stage, of which Aristotle was ignorant. . . ." When this passage is placed in the whole context of its author's thinking, it is clear that the modern writers' "discoveries" were not the result of applying the scientists' method of rational inquiry; rather they were made possible, even inevitable, by changed conditions. "And as our Philosophers have observ'd *Errors* in his PHYSICKS," St. Évremond continues, "our Poets have spy'd out Faults in his POETICKS, at least with respect to Us; considering what great Change all Things have undergone since his Time." He cites as an example of the "great Change all Things have undergone" the contrasting ancient and modern attitudes toward religion.[22]

St. Évremond's concept of progress in the arts thus remained consistent with his critical position of historical relativism. Whatever may be said of Aristotle's errors in physics, his faults in poetics are only so "in respect to Us" who live in altered times. It is clear that this sensitive French nobleman was as responsive to the current idea of progress as any of his English contemporaries. But it is equally clear why it did not lead him, as it did some of them, toward the formulation of a new absolutism in literary criticism: for in the realm of aesthetics at least he regarded it as change rather than improvement. Corneille's "Beauties for the Stage" were other—not greater —than Aristotle's.

Whereas Blackmore felt that modern poetry had fared better than modern poetic theory, John Dennis was among those who thought it a perverse exception to the otherwise universal progress. In *The Advancement and Reformation of Modern Poetry* he begins by reminding his readers that poetry has always been highly esteemed by the great. "And yet," he continues, "to the Confusion of most who have given themselves Time to think of it, Poetry, that has been encourag'd by so many great Princes, is believ'd by several to have degenerated, rather than to have improv'd by Time; while Physicks, Metaphysicks, and some other Arts, that have been very little, or not at all encourag'd, have advanc'd considerably." In the second chapter he declares his conviction that poetry stands to progress as a result of modern extra-literary progress. Like St. Évremond, Dennis does not envision an autonomous poetic progress paralleling that in other fields. Always an environmentalist, he sees rather the progress in science, philosophy, morals, and above all religion, creating the conditions for poetic progress. As for the Ancients,

> They had no Advantage in the Assistance which they receiv'd from the Age in which they writ; on the contrary, the Advantage here, is clearly on the Side of the Moderns: For good Thinking is the Foundation of good Writing, both in Eloquence and in Poetry. Now Thoughts are but the Images of Things, and our Knowledge of Things is greater than that of the Ancients. For several which they knew, are better known to us, and we have several which they never knew at all. How many Arts have the Moderns improv'd? How many wonderful Inventions are owing to them? And how many amazing Discoveries? From which we have a Supply of Thoughts and Images, that is never to be exhausted. So that in the Assistance which we receive, from the Age in which we live, we have the Advantage of the Ancients.

He denies the familiar allegation that the Ancients understood their subjects better than the moderns. "For the Subjects of the Epick, Tragick, and Lyrick Poets, are the Virtues, Vices, and Passions of Men, which the Moderns ought to understand, at least, as well as the Ancients, because they have all the Knowledge of the Ancients, and their own Improvement besides." Man's expanded knowledge of man contributes more to poetic improvement than his expanded knowledge of nature. A decade later, in his notorious attack on Pope's *Essay on Criticism,* Dennis repeats his dual argument in censuring the poet's undue reverence for the classical writers: *they* were not superior in the "natural Powers of the Soul" and *we* have the advantage in experience by living later. And he refers to Bacon's remark about moderns being properly the ancients since they were living in the "elder Ages of the World. . . ."[23]

The one difference between their conceptions of progress accounts for the ultimate significant difference between the critical theories of St. Évremond and Dennis. Both were environmentalists and both saw poetic progress as only a by-product of cultural progress. Yet the older man maintained his position of historical relativism; the younger replaced his by a new absolutism. For St. Évremond conceived of progress as essentially change, Dennis as improvement. More naturally skeptical and less sanguine, the Frenchman believed only that modern men had come upon "new truths"; the Englishman that they had discovered "greater Truth."

But critics like Dryden, St. Évremond, and Dennis, who agreed in sensing the subtleties and complexities of the problem, were perhaps less representative than the many lesser men who made up the "progressive" chorus. Aware only that they were living in stirring times, and intoxicated by the heady wine of discovery and progress, most men were inclined to be impatient of objections and reservations. It seemed inconceivable that literature should not join the triumphant forward march. The past was "a bucket of ashes." Distinctions between the scientific and the aesthetic sounded to them like mere faint-heartedness, to be shouted down along with the now discredited "degenerationism" of the "Ancients."

Samuel Wesley put it appropriately in verse for all his fellow poets.

> Why should we still be lazily *content*
> With thredbare *Schemes,* and nothing *new* invent?
> All *Arts* besides improve, *Sea, Air* and *Land*
> Are every day with *nicer Judgment* scan'd,
> And why should *this* alone be at a stand?
> Or *Nature* largely to the *Ancients* gave
> And little did for *younger Children* save;
> Or rather we *impartial Nature* blame
> To hide our *Sloth,* and cover o'er our *Shame;*
> As *Sinners,* when their *Reason's* drown'd in *Sense,*
> Fall out with *Heav'n,* and quarrel *Providence.*
>     Yet should you our *Galenic Way* despise,
> And some *new Colbatch* of the *Muses* rise;
> No *Quarter* from the *College* hope, who sit
> *Infallible* at *Will's* and judg of *Sense* and *Wit.* . . .

Taken by themselves, these lines could be used to document the case for relativism. But Wesley was no relativist. He urges poets to emulate not only the "newness" of the new science but its absolute method as well.

> Forget not METHOD if the *Prize* you'd gain,
> 'T will cost you *Thought,* but richly pays the *Pain;*
> What *first,* what *second,* or what *last* to place,
> What here will *shine,* and there the *Work* disgrace.[24]

Clearly the "Method" here meant is not the old one of Aristotle; like Colbatch's or Newton's, it is newer and better. And there is no suggestion that it is relative to time, place, or conditions.

# The Idea of Progress

The belief in literary progress was, again, largely a negative support for relativism, anticlassical rather than positively relativist. Samuel Cobb reminds his readers that the "Virtuosi" of Italy, "whose Liberty of Writing and Inventing, enrich'd the Schools and Libraries with gallant Composures" (like Tasso) did so by defying Aristotle's rules. "The Moral is instructive; because to judge well and candidly, we must wean ourselves from a slavish Bigotry to the Ancients. For, tho' Homer and Virgil, Pindar and Horace be laid before us as Examples of exquisite Writing in the Heroic and Lyric Kind, yet, either thro' the Distance of Time, or Diversity of Customs, we can no more expect to find like Capacities, than like Complexions." Here artistic progress is seen to depend not on an emulation of the ways of science but on an abandonment of an inhibiting tradition and an almost Emersonian self-reliance. "Let a Man follow the Talent that Nature has furnish'd him with, and his own Observation has improv'd, we may hope to see Inventions in all Arts, which may dispute Superiority with the best of the Athenian and Roman Excellencies." [25]

Despite the iconoclasm of this "Discourse," the poem "Of Poetry," to which it serves as an introduction, contains only conventional (and patriotic) critical observations: England has outdone, or will outdo, the Ancients; Dryden's "borrowings" are not plagiarisms. Moreover, notwithstanding the environmentalist tone of "Distance of Time, or Diversity of Customs," there is no suggestion that separate criteria of appraisal be applied to classical and English work.

# The Idea of Progress

Another minor writer of the period, Thomas Purney, also bids his fellows to trust to their own "geniuses" as the best way to contribute to poetic progress. He is concerned specifically with the pastoral. "By that means we may hope Pastoral will, one Day, arrive at it's utmost Perfection, which if Writers pretend to go no farther than the first who undertook it (I mean *THEOCRITUS*) it never can do." Purney's argument too implies absolutism, since he believes the progress of a poetic form to be limited, not indefinite. The labor of many men through a certain period of time brings final perfection. "For 'tis no one Genius that can bring any Kind of Poetry to it's greatest Compleatness. And all know by what slow Steps Epick Poetry, Tragedy, and Comedy arrived at the Perfection they now bear." [26]

How one can be sure that a genre has reached this perfection Purney does not make clear. But certainly his reasoning makes no provision for more than one perfect mode. Modern pastoralists are not bidden to invent a new kind of pastoral poem; they are urged to improve upon Theocritus' crude beginnings. When the epitome is finally attained, when later poets have developed the type to its "True Nature," the old Greek and Roman work will logically have to be rated very low in the absolute scale of pastoral excellence.

Yet Purney, as we have seen, was not to be frightened by the hobgoblin of consistency. Aware that some readers appeared to admire Theocritus, he lightly abandons his whole argument by conceding that there may be "several sorts of Pastorals." Similarly, the theory that epic and tragedy arrived gradually "at the Perfection they now bear" is hardly congruous with his declaration that Homer and Milton are "as different as *East* and *West,* yet both excellent," and that *Julius Caesar* and *The Orphan* are of "different sorts." [27] Be that as it may, Purney's belief in poetic progress supported the pervading critical absolutism of his "Enquiry," not its few damaging concessions to relativism.

The conclusion is surely warranted that during this period the study of literature shared with other disciplines the profound impact of the fascinating idea of progress. It provided a rationale for literary history, as part of general human history, and by suggesting that highly developed examples of a genre were the products of a gradual growth from crude origins it stimulated a more careful scrutiny of the literary past. Such scrutiny was frequently motivated by the belief that the true nature of any literary kind might best be grasped by studying its history. Thus Dryden writes of the "Original and Progress of Satire," not as an end in itself but as a means of determining the proper function and characteristics of that kind of poetry.[28]

We may risk a further conclusion as to the effect of progressism upon the absolute-relative debate. The belief in progress, by weakening classical critical dogmatism, provided an opportunity for relativism, but then severely curtailed it by tempting critics to formulate a new absolutism. Owing especially to the course of science, by the overwhelming majority of writers "progress" was interpreted to mean ameliorative development. Ultimately, therefore, the doctrine of progress militated strongly against the first phase of English relativist criticism. In the great literary quarrel, what little relativism there was, was voiced by the "Moderns" for the most part. Yet even that quarrel came to be one principally between opposing groups of absolutists.

That more discriminating view, which saw literary progress not as autonomous, absolute advance, but as the happy by-product of the general intellectual progress, lent more favorable support to relativist theories of appraisal. But only St. Évremond seems to have maintained it consistently.[29] Others tended to pass beyond it in search of new absolute criteria.

# Chapter 7

# The New Absolutism

Like the old absolutism, the new variety sought to establish rules inductively derived from extant literature. It adopted much of Aristotle, Horace, and Longinus—as much as could be squared with modern literary practice. It differed in its awareness of history, that is, in recognizing that literature was shaped in part at least by the cultural conditions surrounding its production, and in its belief in literary progress (variously defined). Whether logically or not, most critics of the neoclassical period were "historical" and "comparative" without being relative. Their absolutism is apparent both when they pass judgment on specific writers and when they expound critical theory.

The work of Dryden's last decade is illustrative. His "Preface to the Fables" (1700) is justly regarded as a discriminating piece of comparative criticism. Moreover, Dryden reveals there his awareness of the influences of their respective cultures and countries upon Ovid, Boccaccio, and Chaucer. And yet he gives the palm at last to the Englishman by the application to all three of one set of criteria. In common with many others, Dryden distinguished between the faults of the age and the faults

of the man. But he insisted that they were faults nonetheless. In "The Original and Progress of Satire" (1693),
he asserts his preference for the satire of Juvenal to that
of Horace. To be sure, he admits, Juvenal's time favored
greater satire, for there were more monstrous vices to in-
vite satirical indignation. "After all, Horace had the dis-
advantage of the times in which he lived; they were better for the man, but worse for the satirist." But, Dryden
observes, "This reflection at the same time excuses Horace, but exalts Juvenal." [1] The critic's task in appraising
literature is to judge, by a single standard, not the talent
but the product. The logic of this combination of historical and absolutist criticism would seem to depend
upon the distinction (which Dryden here makes) between
explaining the faults or virtues of an author's work and
explaining them *away*. The latter Dryden refused to do.
Excellent satire was excellent satire no matter what had
contributed to its excellence. And it is judged to be so
by a universal standard based upon the essence of satire
discovered by studying its exempla throughout history.

It is instructive here to contrast Rapin's procedure in
*De Carmine Pastorali,* made available to English readers
in 1684 by Thomas Creech's translation. He discusses
both Theocritus and Virgil, condemning the Greek by
the standard of the Roman. Theocritus too frequently
violates the "rule" that pastoral love must be free of im-
modesty, suspicion, and loose expressions; Virgil never
does. Rapin is historically conscious, attributing the difference "to their Ages, the times in which the latter liv'd
being more polite, civil, and gentile." [2] But since his cri-

terion of "modest" love is derived from Virgil alone, his absolutism is arbitrary. The method is the reverse of Dryden's: Rapin begins with a definition of pastoral and then proceeds to judge other writers in its light; Dryden begins with the examination and ends with a resulting definition.

Other things being equal, Dryden thought, later work was likely to be better than earlier. But the proviso was important: he was far from the shallow belief that one work was better than another simply because it was written later. He believed only that "good sense is the same in all or most ages; and course of time rather improves Nature, than impairs her . . . another Homer, and another Virgil, may possibly arise from those very causes which produced the first. . . ." This consideration aside, the poetic art, especially within a given genre, was progressive. It is thus neither surprising nor unfair to rate Horace second to Juvenal as a satirist. The younger poet, among other things, had the advantage of "coming after him, and building upon his foundations. . . ." Dryden asks "whether it be any dishonour to Horace to be thus surpassed, since no art or science is at once begun and perfected, but that it must pass first through many hands, and even through several ages. If Lucilius could add to Ennius, and Horace to Lucilius, why, without any diminution to the fame of Horace, might not Juvenal give the last perfection to that work?" [3]

But Dryden's notion of poetic progress diverges in two important respects from those of his less discriminating contemporaries. He contemplated a limited advancement to a perfection at least theoretically attainable, not an indefinite one.[4] Also, in literature at least, he speaks of separate progressive developments in separate cultures. Thus the growth of English prosody from Chaucer through Spenser to Waller and Denham merely paralleled the Roman from Ennius through Virgil and Horace.[5] Like Wotton, Dryden saw clearly that the poet's professional inheritance differed radically in kind from the chemist's.

In this light, it is all the more significant that even its greatest critic could not entirely avoid the predominant tendency of his age to reason from technology to aesthetics. This is especially apparent in his approach to the problem of finding adequate "machines" for the modern epic; for he agreed with those who felt that the pagan religion was happier in this respect than Christianity. "But," he suggests, "what if I venture to advance an invention of my own, to supply the manifest defect of our new writers? I am sufficiently sensible of my weakness; and it is not very probable that I should succeed in such a project, whereof I have not the least hint from any of my predecessors, the poets, or any of their seconds and coadjutors, the critics. Yet we see the art of war is improved in sieges, and new instruments of death are invented daily; something new in philosophy and the mechanics is discovered almost every year; and the science of former ages is improved by the succeeding." Dryden's "invention" is that modern writers may find proper epic "machinery" in the Old Testament. If, he declares, a poet is now living with those rare qualifications of vast

knowledge, natural genius, and mastery of his language
"—if such a man, I say, be now arisen, or shall arise, I
am vain enough to think, that I have proposed a model
to him, by which he may build a nobler, a more beautiful and more perfect poem, than any yet extant since
the Ancients." [6] The poet or the critic, like the engineer,
could "discover" and "invent," but for the improvement
of modern epic only, progress to equal, not to surpass,
the ancient.

Dryden ends his career, then, an absolutist critic, despite a brief flirtation with relativism, when he could ask
himself whether "other ends as suitable to the nature of
tragedy may be found in the English, which were not
in the Greek." [7] It is a new absolutism in that it derives
its theory not from the *Poetics* and *On the Sublime,* but
from literature itself, and in that its practice is to judge
a modern epic or tragedy by the definitions so derived,
not by the *Aeneid* or the *Oedipus Rex.* Historical change
and progress had to be taken into account, but they affected incidentals, not essentials—means, not ends. Homer and Milton had produced variant species of the same
genus.

This process of deriving critical theory from a historical and analytical examination of literature past and
present resulted in the confirmation of the fundamentals of the classical poetic.[8] It ordered, adjusted, cor-
rected; it sometimes cancelled minor classical "rules" and
expanded major ones; [9] but it did not attempt anything
like a wholesale rejection. Its reaffirmation of the car-
dinal Aristotelian and Longinian doctrines was in the

spirit not of Rymer but of Jonson. It suggests that aesthetics does indeed progress, but not in a manner that relegates older systems to a discredited past, possessing only the historical interest that attaches to exploded scientific theories. Rather, it supposes an ideally complete (though perhaps never quite attainable) aesthetic to which each generation may make an ever closer approximation by virtue of having a larger body of literature at its disposal. As his experience of new works leads the critic to make slight "corrective" adjustments of the traditional aesthetic,[10] it may also require minor variations of the position on the scale of excellence held by older masterpieces. Absolutism of this type involves no abandonment of the historical sense; on the contrary, it requires a strong consciousness of the past and the conditions of the past, if only in order to separate the durable from the transient.

This more dynamic (as opposed to dogmatic) absolutism, in which the historical sense becomes the sense of tradition, in which it is the task of each generation of critics to reassess older works and to restate essential theory, has been more consciously defined in the twentieth century in a well-known passage of T. S. Eliot's "Tradition and the Individual Talent."

> No poet, no artist of any art, has his complete meaning alone. His significance, his appreciation is the appreciation of his relation to the dead poets and artists. You cannot value him alone; you must set him, for contrast and comparison, among the dead. I mean this as a principle of aesthetic, not merely historical, criticism . . . what happens when a

new work of art is created is something that happens simultaneously to all the works of art which preceded it. The existing monuments form an ideal order among themselves, which is modified by the introduction of the new . . . work among them. The existing order is complete before the new work arrives; for order to persist after the supervention of novelty, the *whole* existing order must be, if ever so slightly, altered. . . . Whoever has approved this idea of order . . . will not find it preposterous that the past should be altered by the present as much as the present is directed by the past.[11]

Except for his belief that modern Christian poetry might surpass rather than merely equal the ancient, Dennis' position in this regard was similar to Dryden's. His first critical writing displayed the historical relativism examined above; later, he dropped the relativism without however abandoning his sense of historical change. Perhaps more clearly than anyone else, Dennis combined historical analysis with strict absolutist appraisal. In a series of letters published in 1711 under the title of *An Essay on the Genius and Writings of Shakespeare,* he accounts for Shakespeare's "faults" by his times, his lack of knowledge of the rules, and his preoccupation with acting. Dennis' essay, a poor one at best, is certainly not relativist.[12] Like Dryden, he examined new work (notably *Paradise Lost*) in the light of the old, and the old in the light of the new to evolve a critical theory that preserved the essentials of the classical system.

But this was an advance to a new absolutism, not a retreat to authority. For Dennis' eighteenth century critical thought belies his own assertion late in life that the

only known rules are those of Aristotle and his interpreters, unless he was thinking of himself as one of them.
Like so many others, he was impressed by what appeared
to be a discrepancy between the conditions of modern
science and modern literature, especially the drama. The
English, he declared in 1720, have improved in architecture, music, painting, and "the Mechanick Arts" since
the mid-sixteenth century. Only the drama has made no
progress, because playwrights, unlike the practitioners of
these other "arts," have refused to follow the rules. This
dereliction was especially regrettable since, as he saw it,
modern culture provided a better opportunity for producing great poetry than had obtained in ancient times
—thanks above all to Christianity.

Actually, Dennis advances two arguments in support of
the thesis that a Christian culture is uniquely propitious
to poetic creation in the major forms: epic, tragedy, and
what he called the greater ode. One, already noted, is
part of the doctrine of progress: poetry profits by the
advancement of "truth," and Christianity was an obvious advance over paganism in religious truth. This was
a view widely subscribed to, even by some who were
in other respects "Ancients" and classicists.[13] The other,
Dennis' own contribution, belongs in the realm of aesthetic rather than moral criticism. The greatest poetry,
he believed, possessed the quality of the "sublime," and
sublimity could be achieved only in a poem grounded
upon religion.

This argument is not a restatement of the traditional
theory of moral didacticism in pious terms.[14] In order to

be "sublime" a poem had to move passion in the reader, and every rule was valuable to the extent that it contributed to this effect. This passion was itself only a means (though a most important one) to the two ends of poetry, profit and pleasure. "But Passion answers the Two Ends of Poetry better than Harmony can do. . . . For, first, it pleases more, which is evident. . . . And in Tragedy, and in Epick Poetry, a Man may instruct without Harmony, but never without Passion. . . . And as for the greater Ode, if it wants Passion, it becomes hateful and intolerable, and its Sentences grow contemptible." The religious element, in turn, was important as the most effective means of attaining passion—in other words, a means to a means to an end, not the end itself. Its value was aesthetic, not moral. "And thus we have shewn," Dennis writes, "what the chief Excellence in the Body of Poetry is, which we have prov'd to be Passion. Let us now proceed, to the Proofs of what we propounded, That Sacred Subjects, are more susceptible of Passion, than Prophane ones. . . ." [15] And this he proceeds to do at length by examining passages from classical and modern poetry.

Dennis' theory of religion and passion as prime structural elements in poetry is clearly absolute. One notes certain earmarks of the absolutist method in his procedure. His starting point in *The Advancement and Reformation of Modern Poetry* is that found in every absolutist theory—a definition, in this case of poetry itself. "But before we proceed," he writes, "let us define Poetry; which is the first Time that a Definition has been given of that noble Art: For neither Ancient nor Modern Criticks have defin'd Poetry in general. Poetry then is an Imitation of Nature, by a pathetick and numerous Speech." In what immediately follows he distinguishes poetry from prose, concluding that "Poetry is Poetry, because it is more Passionate and Sensual than Prose." Passionless numbers are but measured prose; non-metrical discourse "that is every where extremely pathetick . . . is certainly Poetry without Numbers. . . . Passion then, is the Characteristical Mark of Poetry. . . ." [16]

In two notable respects Dryden and Dennis differed as critics. In the first place, the younger man had higher hopes for the poetic future than the older. Dryden was content with a literary progress which would make modern epic, dramatic, and lyric poets worthy companions to the ancient. Dennis, assured of the value of his own system, hoped for more. Milton, he declared in 1704, had done "better than the best of the Ancients" in the epic; and he would "examine whether it is not possible to advance *English* Tragedy to a greater Height than ever the *Grecian* Poets arriv'd." [17] Secondly, in contrast to Dryden's tentative and occasional speculations, Dennis' work is an attempt at a systematic theory setting forth a poetic in abstract terms. It displays, accordingly, both the merits and the defects of a more ambitious and deliberate undertaking.

These differences between them, however, concern our present purpose less than certain aspects of critical theory in which they agree. Like Dryden's, Dennis' critical system does not displace the Aristotelian-Longinian aesthetic: one does not have to say that if Dennis was right the classical critics were wrong. The *Poetics* seeks primarily to reveal how tragedy functions; *On the Sublime* discovers, among other things, certain formal elements— figures of speech, stylistic devices, organic unity—as absolutes effecting that rare quality of *hypsos* which characterizes the finest literary work. Dennis, agreeing with Longinus that all truly great literature possessed something called "sublimity," sought not a different but a further source of it. In effect, his analysis probes beneath the absolutes of rhetorical detail isolated by Longinus to something he considered more fundamental. In *The Grounds of Criticism,* after paraphrasing Longinus' six "Marks" of the Sublime, he marvels "upon Reflection, how it could happen that so great a Man as *Longinus,* who whenever he met a Passage in any Discourse that was lofty enough to please him, had discernment enough to see that it had some of the preceding Marks, should miss of finding so easy a thing as this, that never any Passage had all these Marks, or so much as the Majority of them, unless it were Religious." [18] Though he departs further from tradition than Dryden and others, his theory is rather an expansion and a complication than a substitution.

Whatever their inherent value,[19] John Dennis' critical writings are of central significance in understanding the nature of the debate between relativist and absolutist as revealed in its first major phase in English criticism. For his work reflects with special fidelity the various and often contradictory influences upon contemporary critical thought of the new science and the new literature, of the idea of progress, and of the growing awareness of history. To dismiss the great bulk of his criticism—and that of his contemporaries—as a willful retreat to authority is to obscure the entire issue.[20] In its failure to see that the one is largely inductive, the other deductive, such a misinterpretation establishes a wholly untenable equation between absolutist and dogmatic criticism. And this confusion, like that between historical and relativist criticism, promotes a misleading simplification of what is in reality a complex problem of literary aesthetics.

# Chapter 8

# Conclusion

English critical relativism is roughly coextensive with the literary criticism of modern times. Contrary to common assumption, it is neither a late "discovery" nor a superior type gradually evolved. Casual and sporadic in the sixteenth and early seventeenth centuries, its arguments became apparent in the writings of almost every critic after the Restoration. Stronger in theory than in practice, and largely negative, it was never predominant. The increasing frequency and force of its claims after the Restoration resulted not in the abolition but in the radical reform of critical absolutism.

Despite an early nexus between them, relativist criticism is neither identical with nor exclusively dependent upon historical criticism. The terms absolute and relative are predicable only of the process of appraisal, to which historical criticism, in the sense of the analysis or elucidation of literature by historical causes, does not address itself. Defined merely as awareness of temporal and local differences, historical criticism is practiced by absolutist and relativist alike. Thomas Rymer for one displayed a knowledge of past literature and a sense of its development. Yet he is notorious as the English exponent of the most rigid neoclassical absolutism. "Founded on reason," his editor writes, "this system was universal and exclusive. It allowed no room for change or development. . . ." [1]

That the relativist position was strengthened in the seventeenth century as inductive science replaced ancient authority has long been recognized. Some have therefore mistaken the persistence of ancient doctrines in literary theory as a uniquely reactionary deference to classical authority by men of letters. This assumes a fallacy common in the period under discussion: that aesthetic theory progresses like scientific. More important, by identifying absolutism with authoritarianism, it supposes that ancient literary theory escaped the rational scrutiny applied to the rest of ancient learning during the late Renaissance; whereas the opposite can easily be proved. Although the new science discredited authority, it ultimately favored absolutism. Its spokesmen insisted that their success was owing to the use of an objective and universally valid method. And the "truth" thus discovered was equally absolute. Along with political, ethical, and religious thinkers, literary critics felt the pervasive influence of the "mathematicism" characteristic of the age. Like its byproduct, the idea of progress, the scientific movement prepared the ground for relativist concepts by weakening ancient authority. Its fundamental premises, however, were inimical to relativism itself.

Examination of the early relativist elements in our criticism helps to clarify the entire issue. Most important perhaps, it shows that the very phrase "relative-

# Conclusion

versus-absolute" fosters an obscuring oversimplification. Throughout the period surveyed we discern four rather than two broad theoretical positions: two absolutisms and two relativisms. At irreconcilable extremes from each other are the theory of personal taste (since called impressionism) and what I have called means-and-end absolutism. Neither bears examination. The first has frequently been dismissed as negating the possibility of any feasible aesthetic at all. Less facile and perhaps more damning is the objection that it fails to recognize, let alone account for, the rough consensus toward certain works or authors prevalent during any period, and in some cases perennial. Absolutism of means and end, sounder theoretically, fails in application. Divorcing the literary work from its cultural matrix and therefore confounding the essential with the accidental, this critical literalism inevitably produces insensate praise or blame. It led Rymer to absurdities that were fair game for Samuel Butler's satirical barbs.[2]

Other relativists, eschewing impressionism, held to objective standards but argued that these must vary with circumstances of time and place. This better relativism produced the better absolutism. By their emphasis on the unique as against the universal, their conception of literary works as contextual resultants, and their salutary pragmatism, critics of this persuasion forced the discrimination of means and ends. The common ascription of Rymer's ridiculous treatment of Shakespeare to a lack of critical sensibility is at best a partial explanation. It would be hard to show that Dennis, whose reputation is higher, was better endowed in this respect. But it is even less valid to impute Rymer's poor showing to critical absolutism. For this reasoning becomes paradoxical when it is considered that Dryden, critically the zenith to Rymer's nadir, also applied absolute criteria in his best criticism. The paradox disappears only in the light of a clear distinction between the absolutisms of end and of means and end.

If few today would defend rigid absolutism, the evidence declares as well against the possibility of a valid and workable relativist aesthetic. Relativist concepts in the first phase of the debate did create a more responsible absolute aesthetic by destroying the means-and-end dogmatism. But a stronger claim can hardly be supported. Our finest criticism since has been nonauthoritarian, but absolute, because good criticism requires what the relativist has never been able to provide: a basis in theory. Lacking this, evaluative pronouncements remain mere expressions of opinion, however enlightened; with it, they become systematic and therefore intelligible discourse. Extreme absolutism can do this, to be sure. But the more adaptable kind, admitting variable means, can do more; as surely as any relativism, it guards against those neat and exclusive formulae by which a book is censured for not being what it could not be or was not meant to be. It is an effective antidote to Rymerism. And the ghost of Rymer haunts every age.

# Notes

### NOTES TO THE FOREWORD

1. "The Relative and the Absolute: An Exchange of Views," *Sewanee Review,* LVII (1949), 357-377.
2. *Theory of Literature,* p. 35.
3. Introduction to *Critics and Criticism Ancient and Modern,* p. 11.


### NOTES TO CHAPTER 1

1. See, for example, G. M. Miller's *The Historical Point of View in English Literary Criticism from 1570-1770,* esp. pp. 34-35; Francis Gallaway's *Reason, Rule, and Revolt in English Classicism,* p. 286; U. J. P. Rushton's "The Development of Historical Criticism in England 1532-1700," p. 46.
2. A typical example is John Dennis' "The Characters and Conduct of Sir John Edgar," *The Critical Works of John Dennis,* ed. E. N. Hooker (hereinafter cited as Hooker), II, 197-198.
3. Yet the tendency to restrict the term "historical" to relativist criticism persists: "Only when standards are thoroughly relative can we have historical criticism . . ." (Donald M. Foerster, *Homer in English Criticism,* p. 9). It may rather be questioned whether any criticism,

relative or otherwise, which ignores the historical setting of its object can ever be wholly adequate. "The
critic," as one aesthetician has put it, "seeks to re-create
the individual work of art with true artistic sensitivity,
and to do this he must set it in its historical context"
(Theodore Meyer Greene, *The Arts and the Art of Criticism*, p. 22). And Greene's aesthetic is not relativist.
(See his chapter on "Artistic Greatness," pp. 461-478.)

4. "Dryden," *Lives of the English Poets by Samuel Johnson,
   Ll.D.*, I, 475.
5. René Wellek thinks that "neither the theory of taste nor
   relativism, which has frequently been misnamed the
   'historical point of view,' were in themselves directly
   favourable to the rise of literary history" (*The Rise of
   English Literary History*, p. 25).
6. *The Idiom of Poetry*, p. 47.

## NOTES TO CHAPTER 2

1. See George Saintsbury, "Elizabethan Criticism," *CHEL*,
   III, 351.
2. *Elizabethan Critical Essays* (hereinafter cited as Smith),
   Introd., pp. xxxvii, lxi.
3. "The Scholemaster," Smith, I, 29-34.
4. Smith, I, 6.
5. Justification of the doctrine of *Imitatio* depends of course
   on some kind of absolutism. "This *Imitatio* is *dissimilis
   materiei similis tractatio;* and, also, *similis materiei dissimilis tractatio,* as *Virgill* followed *Homer:* but the argument to the one was *Ulysses,* to the other *Aeneas.
   Tullie* persecuted *Antonie* with the same wepons of
   eloquence that *Demosthenes* used before against *Phi-
   lippe*" (Smith, I, 8). For both genres there is an essential element. Differences of time, circumstances, lan-

guage, etc., have no bearing on the essence of eloquence, persuasion; neither do they affect the essence
of the epic, whose purpose is to inculcate the virtues
of courage and loyalty.

6. *A History of Criticism and Literary Taste in Europe*, II,
   157. Pp. 157-162 give an account of the beginnings of
   this movement in England. Cf. J. E. Spingarn's *A History of Literary Criticism in the Renaissance*, pp. 298-
   304.

7. Smith, I, 117-118.

8. Smith, I, 144, 137, 141.

9. Smith, I, 266, 274.

10. Smith, I, 278, 279.

11. Puttenham is aware of the inconsistency himself. Cf.
    Smith, II, 17.

12. Smith, II, 16-24, 71-72. He is inconsistent on this point
    too. Cf. II, 121: ". . . I sayd it in a sort truly, but now
    I must recant. . . ."

13. Smith, II, 80-81.

14. Smith, II, 10-11.

15. Smith, II, 240. It is possible that Nash's real position lies
    beyond historical relativism, that he was at bottom com-
    pletely skeptical. For in his preface to Sidney's *Astro-
    phel and Stella* (1591) he remarks that "our opinion (as
    *Sextus Empiricus* affirmeth) gives the name of good or
    ill to every thing," and mentions a recent English trans-
    lation of the Greek philosopher's works. Louis I. Bred-
    vold, in a chapter of his *Intellectual Milieu of John
    Dryden* entitled "The Traditions of Skepticism," writes:
    "In these treatises [of Empiricus] the Renaissance found
    the most thorough and systematic demonstration yet at-
    tempted of the relativity of all knowledge, and of the
    futility of philosophizing" (p. 18).

16. Saintsbury, *A History of Criticism,* II, 187.

17. Smith, II, 333.

18. Smith, II, 330.

19. Smith, II, 359.

# Notes

20. Smith, II, 384, 363.
21. Smith, II, 364.
22. Throughout the *Defence* there is a subtle appeal to patriotism and national pride. A. C. Sprague says that the "Defence" combines a sense of history and of human progress "with a love of England and of England's past" (*Samuel Daniel: Poems and A Defence of Ryme*, Introd., p. xxiii).
23. Smith, II, 359-360.
24. Some readers may prefer to call "end-only" absolutists "relativists of means." This seems legitimate enough, but most writers have placed them with the absolutists.
25. Smith, II, 359.
26. J. W. H. Atkins, *English Literary Criticism: The Renascence*, p. 199.
27. Saintsbury, "Elizabethan Criticism," *CHEL*, III, 333.
28. "A Preface, or rather a Briefe Apologie of Poetrie . . ." (introductory to his 1591 translation of *Orlando Furioso*), Smith, II, 215.
29. Smith, II, 212, 213.
30. *English Literary Criticism: The Renascence*, p. 194.
31. Smith, II, 175.

## NOTES TO CHAPTER 3

1. Richard F. Jones, for example, argues that literary theory was authoritarian at the very time when science was anti-authoritarian. "Here, then, was a critical philosophy which upheld the principle of authority (though many critics tried to equate it with reason or common sense). . . . It would be difficult to find a more exact antithesis to the views characteristic of the scientific movement than is found in this criticism" ("Science and

# Notes

Criticism in the Neo-Classical Age of English Literature," *JHI,* I [October 1940], 383).

2. As does Jones, who calls Dryden "the very Janus of critics," sometimes dogmatic, sometimes skeptical and inductive. "The method of reasoning employed by the
dogmatic critics of his day was essentially deductive or
syllogistic. They reasoned from general principles established largely by authority" ("Science and Criticism
. . . ," p. 385). And W. P. Ker, who says of Dryden's
preface to *Troilus and Cressida* (1679): "There is rather
more constraint in this essay, more obsequious respect
for authorities, than is common with Dryden . . ." (*Essays of John Dryden* [hereinafter cited as Ker], Introd.,
I, lxii).

3. Aphorism 61, Book I, *Novum Organum.* He leaves the
Ancients in possession of their honors, but adds: "The
lame . . . in the path outstrip the swift, who wander
from it, and it is clear that the very skill and swiftness
of him who runs not in the right direction, must increase his aberration.

"Our method of discovering the sciences is such as
to leave little to the acuteness and strength of wit, and
indeed rather to level wit and intellect. For, as in the
drawing of a straight line or accurate circle by the
hand, much depends upon its steadiness and practice,
but if a ruler or compass be employed there is little
occasion for either; so it is with our method" (*Works,*
III, 350). This notion, applied to literary criticism, persisted throughout the century. Sir Richard Blackmore,
in 1695, explains the failure of the moderns to produce
an epic: "That the modern Poets have been so unsuc-
cessful has not, I imagin, proceeded so much from want
of *Genius* as from Ignorance of the Rules of writing
such a Poem, or at least from their want of attending
to them" (*Critical Essays of the Seventeenth Century,*
ed. J. E. Spingarn [hereinafter cited as Spingarn], III,
234).

# Notes

4. "A Dissertation Concerning the Perfection of the English Language, and the State of Poetry, &c.," *Critical Essays of the Eighteenth Century 1700-1725,* ed. Willard Durham (hereinafter cited as Durham), pp. 365-366, 367.
5. Spingarn, Introd., p. xc.
6. This dialectic was convenient in many ways. Puritanical or moralistic writers, for instance, found in it a means of dealing with Horace's troublesome *aut prodesse aut delectare.* The Christian didacticism of the Renaissance (e.g., Sidney's *Apology*) regularly strained the Latin syntax to make the second term instrumental to the first: to instruct by pleasing. But a century later the equally moral Blackmore could put the matter in abstract terms by then familiar: "'T is true, indeed, that one End of Poetry is to give Men Pleasure and Delight; but this is but a subordinate, subaltern End, which is it self a Means to the *greater* and *ultimate* one before mention'd" ("Preface to *Prince Arthur, an Heroick Poem*" [1695], Spingarn, III, 229). Even Jeremy Collier thought in terms of ends and means. He argued that comedy was properly as moral as tragedy because "it does not differ from *Tragedy* in the End, but in the *Means.* . . . The one works by Terror, the other by Infamy . . . but they meet in the same point at last" ("A Short View . . . of the English Stage" [1698], Spingarn, III, 264).
7. "Preface to Rapin," Spingarn, II, 165.
8. Professor Pottle, who finds literary criticism traditionally absolutist, writes: "Literary criticism seems always to have resembled 'classical' physics. From the time of Aristotle to the present day, critics must have believed in the possibility of absolute judgments, for they have always been making them" (*The Idiom of Poetry,* p. 10). It is interesting to note that in defending his relativist method Pottle points to the modern scientific relativity of Eddington and Einstein and asks: "Would it not be well, with this example of the scientists before us, if

we looked at the critics' standard or measure to assure
ourselves that it is an unchanging scale, or, if it varies,
that the variations are of a kind that can be predicted
and allowed for?"

9. *An Essay Concerning Human Understanding*, p. 277. On
the pervasive influence of "mathematicism" during this
period see Basil Willey, *The Eighteenth Century Background*, p. 23, and W. J. Bate, *From Classic to Romantic*, pp. 25-29.
10. "Mythomystes," Spingarn, I, 144-145, 149.
11. *The Tragedies of the Last Age* (1678), p. 3.
12. "Timber: or, Discoveries," *Ben Jonson*, VIII, 637.
13. *Miscellanea: or Various Discourses . . . By the Seiur de
Saint Evremont . . . made English By Ferrand Spence*,
"The Preface," [no pag.].
14. *The Tragedies of the Last Age*, p. 5.
15. "The Grounds of Criticism in Poetry" (1704), Hooker, I,
335. Cf. "We have said above, that as Poetry is an Art,
it must have a certain End, and that there must be
Means that are proper for the attaining that End, which
Means are otherwise call'd the Rules" (I, 336).
16. Hooker, I, 331.
17. "The Causes of the Decay and Defects of Dramatick Poetry . . ." (1725?), Hooker, II, 283.
18. Durham, p. 49.
19. Durham, pp. 62, 65, 67.
20. Durham, pp. 60, 61.
21. "Preface to Albion and Albanius," Ker, I, 271-272.
22. "Defence of an Essay of Dramatic Poesy" (1668), Ker, I,
123. Hoyt Trowbridge has recently written of this passage: "This argument assumes that an art is a skill directed to some end and that the existence of an end
implies some means of attaining it. Rules of poetic production, formulating the means appropriate to attaining the poet's end, are therefore inherent in the nature of poetry as an art; and these same rules provide the standards by which the products of his art

# Notes

are to be judged" ("The Place of the Rules in Dryden's Criticism," *MP*, XLIV [November 1946], 88-89). Trowbridge's article argues further that for Dryden these means were probable, not dogmatic or certain. The exceptions to this generalization, shown above, though few, are at least historically significant.

23. "A Parallel of Poetry and Painting," Ker, II, 134.

24. To state this in other terms, there was no quarrel about the *definitions* of these genres. But extreme relativism necessarily involves the notion of more than one equally valid definition, terms like epic, tragedy, novel, and so forth being mere labels of convenience. Definitions (which in literary aesthetics are usually function-descriptions) are more than incidentally related to appraisal; they appear to me crucial. "It has rather recently been discovered," writes Stephen C. Pepper, "that definitions are the ultimate basis of judgments of value. Men used to think of norms as the basis, which was right enough except that norms have to be defined; or they would think of authority as the basis, such as the fiat of an expert, or a deity, or a man's inner aesthetic taste, which again, however, required a definition to indicate the expert, the deity, or the bounds of aesthetic taste. We now clearly see that the basis of the whole matter is a definition" (*The Basis of Criticism in the Arts*, p. 25). Herbert J. Muller, an able exponent of relativism, has to admit that "men continue to talk and think in terms of essences. They seek definitions—as of poetry—on the assumption that a single or absolute quality is involved" (*Science and Criticism*, p. 21). Cleanth Brooks, a modern absolutist, also sees a close relationship between critical appraisal and definition. He feels that "in giving up our criteria of good and bad, we have, as a consequence . . . begun to give up our concept of poetry itself. Obviously, if we can make no judgments about a poem *as* a *poem*, the concept of poetry as distinct from other

138

kinds of discourse which employ words becomes meaningless" ("Criticism, History and Critical Relativism," *The Well Wrought Urn,* p. 198).

25. "Timber: or, Discoveries," *Ben Jonson,* VIII, 624.
26. Spingarn, II, 264-265.
27. "Answer to Davenant's Preface," Spingarn, II, 57.
28. "The Author's Apology for Heroic Poetry and Poetic License, Prefixed to 'The State of Innocence and Fall of Man,' an Opera" (1677), Ker, I, 189.
29. Ed. Edith J. Morley, p. 11.
30. "Preface to the Reader" (1610-1616?), Spingarn, I, 72. By the end of the century this idea had become a critical commonplace. Cf. Roscommon's "An Essay on Translated Verse" (1684):

> Words in One Language Elegantly us'd
> Will hardly in another be excus'd,
> And some that Rome admir'd in *Caesars* Time
> May neither suit *Our Genius* nor our *Clime.*
> (Spingarn, II, 303.)

31. "To the Reader," Spingarn, I, 77. For an account of the theory of translation in the seventeenth century, see Spingarn's Introd., pp. xlviii-lviii.
32. "Preface to the Translation of Ovid's Epistles" (1680), Ker, I, 239, 241 (italics mine). Cf. "Preface to Sylvae" (1685), Ker, I, 252.
33. As early as the "Essay of Dramatic Poesy" (1668) Dryden raises the question. He sees it as a limitation on modern competency to appraise ancient "wit." Eugenius admits that moderns must in part suspend judgment "because, the languages being dead, and many of the customs and little accidents on which it depended lost to us, we are not competent judges of it." The statement is however qualified by his remark that "a thing well said will be wit in all languages . . ." (Ker, I, 51). Dryden apparently felt that any modern epic was doomed to an absolute though slight inferiority because of its

language. In "The Original and Progress of Satire" (1693), he argues that any age may produce a literary genius equal to the ancient, "abating only for the language" (Ker, II, 25). Further on he says that a modern epic may equal the ancient except that the language would not be "of equal dignity, yet as near approaching to it, as our modern barbarism will allow, which is all that can be expected from our own, or any other now extant, though more refined; and therefore we are to rest contented with that only inferiority, which is not possible to be remedied" (Ker, II, 31).

34. Ker, II, 215, 228.

35. "The Preface to *Sejanus, His Fall*" (1605), Spingarn, I, 10.

36. Ker, I, 55.

37. "Preface to *Four New Plays*" (1665), Spingarn, II, 98, 99-100.

38. "Dryden," *Lives of the English Poets by Samuel Johnson*, I, 478 (italics mine).

39. "Preface Containing the Grounds of Criticism in Tragedy" (1679), Ker, I, 211 (italics mine).

40. Ker, I, 123, 124.

41. "The Author's Preface to His Much Honour'd Friend Mr. Hobs" (1650), Spingarn, II, 9. The complex and fascinating problem of the "modern" epic has received excellent treatment in Basil Willey's *The Seventeenth Century Background,* Chap. X, "The Heroic Poem in a Scientific Age." (See esp. "The Climate of Opinion," pp. 205-219.)

42. Ker, I, 160.

43. "The Original . . . of Satire" (1693), Ker, II, 101-102. Here again, Homer's "rudeness" is not being condemned. The metaphor of clothing styles supports the reading that Dryden is arguing for recognition of change, not belief in "progress."

44. Hooker, I, 30. Noting the theoretical similarity of Dryden's and Dennis' objections to Rymer's method,

# Notes

Hooker mentions the means-and-end technique as central to their argument (I, 445).

45. "To My Honoured and Ingenious Friend Mr. *Harrington,* for the Modern Poets Against the Ancients" (1694), Durham, pp. 16-17. This passage provides illustration for a *caveat.* Contrary to first appearances, the terms of the well-known critical controversy, "Ancient" and "Modern," are not interchangeable with "absolutist" and "relativist." True, an "Ancient" was almost certain to be absolutist in theory, but a "Modern" could be either. And the *via media* of relativism of means was especially double-edged, in that it was employed, with equal logic, against absolutist and relativist alike. In this passage Gildon is clearly attacking ultra-conservative absolutism (absolutism of means and end).

46. Francis Gallaway, *Reason, Rule, and Revolt in English Classicism,* p. 286.

## NOTES TO CHAPTER 4

1. "The Relative and the Absolute: An Exchange of Views" (with Cleanth Brooks), *Sewanee Review,* LVII (1949), 358.

2. *The Basis of Criticism in the Arts,* p. 68.

3. "Il n'y a pas plus de critique objective qu'il n'y a d'art objectif," wrote Anatole France. . . . "Pour être franc, le critique devrait dire:—Messieurs, je vais parler de moi à propos de Shakespeare, à propos de Racine, ou de Pascal, ou de Goethe" (*La Vie Littéraire,* Première Série, p. iii).

   Do readers of Pater's *Renaissance* really learn about Renaissance art or about Pater? Oscar Wilde declared that the best criticism was "creative," the ostensible subject of any critique being a mere point of departure, an "occasion" as it were, for a new creative work by the critic.

4. Paul Spencer Wood, "The Opposition to Neo-Classicism in England between 1660 and 1700," *PMLA,* XLIII (March 1928), 195.

5. "Dryden," *Lives of the English Poets by Samuel Johnson,* I, 473, 474.

6. *A History of Criticism,* II, 397n.

7. "Of Ancient and Modern Tragedy," *The Works of Monsieur De St. Evremond made English from the French Original . . . by Mr. Des Maizeaux,* II, 12, 13.

8. Hooker, I, 11-12.

9. "Their women under so warm a Sun," Dennis observes, "melted much sooner than ours" (Hooker, I, 12). He probably derived this idea from St. Évremond.

10. "The conception of the 'time spirit' has also frequently disastrous consequences for a conception of the continuity of Western civilization: the individual ages are conceived as far too sharply distinct and discontinuous, and the revolutions which they show are conceived of as so radical that the *Geisteswissenschaftler* ends not only in complete historical relativism (one age is as good as another) but also in a false conception of individuality and originality which obscures the basic constants in human nature, civilization, and the arts. In Spengler we arrive at the idea of closed cultural cycles developing with fatal necessity: self-enclosed, though mysteriously parallel" (Wellek and Warren, *Theory of Literature,* pp. 120-121).

11. Hooker, I, 22.

12. "Remarks on a Book Entituled, Prince Arthur, an Heroick Poem, with Some Critical Observations, and Several New Remarks upon Virgil" (1696), Hooker, I, 60.

13. "The Advancement and Reformation of Modern Poetry" (1701), Hooker, I, 265-266.

14. "Some Reflections on Mr. Rymer's Short View of Tragedy, and an Attempt at a Vindication of Shakespeare,

in an Essay directed to John Dryden Esq . . . ," *Miscellaneous Letters and Essays, on Several Subjects* . . . , pp. 67-68, 86, 76-77, 170.

15. *Miscellaneous Letters and Essays,* p. 150.

16. Critics who disagreed about other things frequently held the common view that English character was peculiar in its "humour," and that this accounted for the peculiar bent of English comic drama. Temple believed that modern English drama surpassed the ancient because of its "humours," which he traced to the peculiar political, economic, and social conditions of life ("Of Poetry," Spingarn, III, 103-104). Congreve, in a letter to Dennis, records his agreement with Temple. He does not "wonder at" that abundance of "humour" in English comedy, "for I look upon Humour to be almost of English growth; at least, it does not seem to have found such Encrease on any other Soil. And what appears to me to be the reason of it is the greater Freedom, Privilege, and Liberty which the Common People of *England* enjoy" ("*Mr.* Congreve *to Mr.* Dennis, *Concerning Humour in Comedy,*" Spingarn, III, 252).

17. "A Discourse upon Comedy, in Reference to the English Stage" (1702), Durham, p. 264.

18. Durham, pp. 275, 275-276, 277.

19. *A Full Enquiry into the True Nature of Pastoral* (1717), p. 71.

20. "Preface to *The Great Favourite, or the Duke of Lerma*" (1668), Spingarn, II, 106.

21. "Defence of an Essay," Ker, I, 120-121.

22. *The Aesthetic Theory of Thomas Hobbes,* p. 122.

23. See Louis I. Bredvold, *The Intellectual Milieu of John Dryden,* Introd., pp. 11-15.

24. Spingarn, III, 62.

25. For example, the notion of *le bon goût* in France. See Atkins, *English Literary Criticism: 17th and 18th Centuries,* p. 29.

26. A. Bosker, *Literary Criticism in the Age of Johnson,* p. 18.

# Notes

27. "To my Honoured and Ingenious Friend Mr. *Harring-ton,* for the Modern Poets against the Ancients," Durham, p. 15.
28. "The Preface," The Eighth Edition (1737), [no pag.].
29. *A Pastoral Poem on the Victories at Schellenburg and Blenheim . . . with a Large Preface, Shewing the Antiquity and Dignity of Pastoral Poetry . . .* [no pag.].
30. Durham, p. 106.
31. "A Defence of Sir Fopling Flutter, a Comedy Written by Sir George Etheridge" (1722), Hooker, II, 244.
32. *An Enquiry into the Life and Writings of Homer,* The Second Edition, pp. 288, 287.


NOTES TO CHAPTER 5

1. Spingarn, II, 81.
2. Frances Willard Hadley finds that the notions of race and climate were merged in English criticism ("The Theory of Milieu in English Criticism from 1660 to 1801").
3. Ker, I, 72. Interesting to note, in connection with a point made in the previous chapter, is that Neander immediately shifts his defense of the English dramatists to an absolutist basis, declaring that "it is unnatural for anyone in a great passion to speak long together . . ."
4. "Of Comedy," *Miscellanea: or Various Discourses,* pp. 11-20, 15.
5. "Of the English Comedy," *Miscellanea: or Various Discourses,* p. 33.
6. "Preface to *The Court of Death*" (1695), Hooker, I, 42, 43.
7. "The Answer of Mr. Hobbes to Sr Will. D'Avenant's *Preface* Before *Gondibert*" (1650), Spingarn, II, 62.
8. "Preface to *Poems*" (1656), Spingarn, II, 89.
9. "The Original . . . of Satire" (1693), Ker, II, 30-31. Boileau's *L'Art Poétique,* published in 1674, had been

translated by Dryden and Sir William Soame[s] and published in 1683.

10. "Of Poetry," Spingarn, III, 99.

11. It was also, curiously enough, suggestive to some of idolatry. In "An Apology for Poetry, in an Essay Directed to Walter Moil Esq . . ." Gildon argued that the modern poets' use of pagan deities does not imply false worship since "they only employ them as the Vehicles of their Designs" (*Miscellaneous Letters and Essays*, p. 37).

12. "Preface to Prince Arthur, an Heroick Poem" (1695), Spingarn, III, 239-240.

13. "An Essay upon Epick Poetry," *Essays upon Several Subjects*, p. 74. Blackmore makes this point only of the epic. In his Appendix to this essay he declares that the tragic poets may do otherwise. In tragedy the characters speak for themselves; in epic the poet speaks in his own right (p. 183).

14. "The Grounds of Criticism in Poetry" (1704), Hooker, I, 369.

15. "Preface to *The Battle of Ramillia*" (1706), Hooker, I, 394. Cf. his exception to Pope's statement in the *Preface to Homer* that Homer's gods are the gods of poetry. No one, Dennis objects, can now write a successful epic with heathen "machines" ("Remarks upon the Dunciad" [1729], Hooker, II, 369).

16. "*Observations on the* Paradise Lost *of Milton*," Letter III of the "Letters on Milton and Wycherley" (1721-1722), Hooker, II, 228-229.

17. *Theory of Literature*, p. 101.

18. "Preface to *Poems*" (1656), Spingarn, II, 89. Cowley's complaint was not uncommon throughout the neoclassical period. See Gallaway, *Reason, Rule, and Revolt in English Classicism*, p. 214.

19. Ker, I, 99.

20. Here seventeenth century criticism takes note of a notion that has received special attention in the twentieth. In a recent comment on this passage D. N. Smith

quotes Robert Bridges writing in 1912 on Milton's exhaustion of blank verse (*John Dryden,* p. 6). What is perhaps the modern *locus classicus* is T. E. Hulme's version of it in "Romanticism and Classicism" (*Speculations,* pp. 121-122).

21. "An Essay of Dramatic Poesy" (1668), Ker, I, 99.
22. "John Dryden, Esq.," *An Account of the English Dramatick Poets* (1691), in Spingarn, III, 125-126. A less helpful use of this idea was as an excuse by a writer for his own faults. Oldmixon declared that he had written in rhyme rather than in blank verse only in "Compliance to the Taste of the Age." He looked to a "second *Milton*" to carry on the fight against rhyme, a "barbarous Yoke, impos'd on the Muses in the Ages of Darkness and Ignorance" (*A Pastoral Poem . . . with a Large Preface . . .* [no pag.] ). The argument is weak, but it is further evidence of a recognition of the force of the literary "climate."
23. "The Advancement and Reformation of Modern Poetry" (1701), Hooker, I, 246.
24. Note that this involves the need for a further distinction. Appraisal of two authors might find their talents, i.e., their accomplishments, equal, while maintaining that the writings of one were superior to the other's because his age was more favorable to the composition of the kind of things both attempted. Dryden's awareness of this distinction is discussed in Chapter 7.
25. "Some Reflections on Mr. Rymer's Short View of Tragedy, and an Attempt at a Vindication of Shakespeare . . . ," *Miscellaneous Letters and Essays,* pp. 88-89.
26. Second Edition (1697), pp. 4-5.
27. Second Edition (1736), pp. 288, 289.
28. Bosker's observation that the "eighteenth century saw the dawn of the sociological method" (*Literary Criticism in the Age of Johnson,* p. 61) surely wants revision, as does his conclusion that "the pseudo-classical belief in absolute standards had been greatly shaken in the second

# Notes

half of the eighteenth century." That belief had received many a shock by 1700.

29. *English Literature and Society in the Eighteenth Century,* p. 20.
30. "The Original . . . of Satire" (1693), Ker, II, 25.
31. Spingarn, III, 208-209, 210.
32. Spingarn, III, 210.
33. The distinction between the two positions, though perhaps only one of degree, is important. Blackmore too had felt that the Greek and Roman epics could not be imitated effectively under modern conditions. But the genre itself transcended circumstances of time and place. Decrying the modern poets' enslavement to the ancient models, he wrote: ". . . I express'd my Wishes that some great Genius . . . would break the Ice, assert the Liberty of Poetry . . . would attempt an Epick Poem, in some measure, of a different Cast, but agreeable however to the Nature and Constitution of that Species of Poetry; such as might bear a Conformity to the Taste of the present Times, and to the Customs, Manners, and Establish'd Religion of the Author's Country" ("An Appendix" to "An Essay upon Epick Poetry," *Essays upon Several Subjects,* p. 156).
34. Spingarn, III, 211.
35. "The Causes of the Decay and Defects of Dramatick Poetry . . ." (1725?), Hooker, II, 297.


NOTES TO CHAPTER 6

1. *The Idea of Progress,* p. 7.
2. An extended analysis of this idea may be found in R. F. Jones' *Ancients and Moderns.* (See esp. Chap. II, "The Decay of Nature.") See also Bury's "The Doctrine of Degeneration: The Ancients and Moderns," *Idea of*

*Progress,* pp. 78-97. Students of Milton will recall the poet's early argument against it (whether serious or not) in *Naturam non Pati Senium.*

3. *Ancients and Moderns,* p. 23. Perhaps the latter part of this statement accords to the decay idea more than its due. In any case it suggests an unwarranted simplification. Many of course felt that the Ancients were superior because they came first. But the reasoning ran both ways. The undeniable excellence of ancient thought seemed to confirm the theory. Cf. Bury, *Idea of Progress,* p. 33.

4. Spingarn, I, 128, 144.

5. *Idea of Progress,* pp. 79, 109-110. Cf. Atkins, *English Literary Criticism: The Renascence,* p. 360; Gallaway, *Reason, Rule, and Revolt in English Classicism,* p. 191; Jones, *Ancients and Moderns,* p. 23; Burlingame, *The Battle of the Books in Its Historical Setting,* pp. 178-181.

6. "An Essay upon the Ancient and Modern Learning" (1690), Spingarn, III, 50, 55. In no sense original with Temple, the cyclic theory of civilization is traceable to ancient times, and was familiar to the learned men of his day. But the interpretation he gave it, Marburg observes, caught the interest of both English and French writers and scientists concerned with the possibility of human progress (*Sir William Temple,* p. 45).

7. It consists perfectly well with the relativist view. In his anti-absolutist "Dissertation Concerning the Perfection of the English Language . . ." Leonard Welsted took the position that culture does not improve indefinitely. It reaches a peak, decays, and then repeats the process elsewhere. He instances Rome, relating the linguistic decay to the political and military ruin (Durham, pp. 359-361). "Thus has *Learning,* in different Ages, shifted her Abode, deserting one People to cultivate another . . ." (p. 361).

8. A few, including Fontenelle, had reservations about it; Pascal protested unheeded. (See Bate, *From Classic to Romantic,* p. 33.) H. W. Taeusch accords Wotton principal credit for establishing the modern separation of the arts and sciences ("The Influence of the Idea of Progress on English Literary Criticism to 1700"). It is inaccurate to say that the concept of artistic progress sprang entirely from the analogy with scientific progress. Bosker traces it to the *Querelle* in France, where the "Moderns" seized upon it as convenient for their argument (*Literary Criticism in the Age of Johnson,* p. 51). But it had been already implied in the earlier Italian thesis of general human progress, as Spingarn suggests (Spingarn, Introd., p. lxxxix).

9. "Reflections upon Monsieur Perrault's Hypothesis, That Modern Orators and Poets are more excellent than Ancient" (Chap. IV of *Reflections upon Ancient and Modern Learning*), Spingarn, III, 220, 218. Wotton put philosophy in the same category with poetry and oratory. Bury stresses another basis for his dichotomy between art and science. The sciences (knowledge) are cumulative because independent of conditions, whereas the arts, dependent on conditions, may decline or even disappear (*Idea of Progress,* pp. 121-122). For this, though, Wotton himself plainly offered another reason, the vagaries of taste: ". . . Mankind loves Variety in those Things wherein it may be had so much that the best Things, constantly re-iterated, will certainly disgust" (Spingarn, III, 218).

10. *De Re Poetica* . . . , p. 12. Norris included religion and music among "arts" that strangely failed to progress (p. 13).

11. "Timber: or, Discoveries," *Ben Jonson,* VIII, 627.

12. "Preface to *Gondibert*" (1650), Spingarn, II, 2, 7, 20.

13. Pottle believes that the commonest assumption underlying absolutist critical theory is "the assumption of a progression of taste, of an accumulation of critical

knowledge which makes the later age always more clear-sighted." And this, he adds, means that critical doctrine has improved steadily from Elizabethan times, that T. S. Eliot is sounder than Arnold, who is sounder than Coleridge, and so forth. "In science that would be just what one would find, for science is progressive. Though one would hesitate to say that anybody was or ever would be a greater scientific genius than Sir Isaac Newton, we should expect the scientific theories of Faraday and Maxwell to be 'sounder' than Newton's. . . . Science cumulates, criticism does nothing of the sort" (*The Idiom of Poetry*, p. 28).

14. "To My Honoured and Ingenious Friend Mr. *Harrington,* for the Modern Poets against the Ancients" (1694), Durham, pp. 14-15.

15. "Some Reflections on Mr. Rymer's Short View of Tragedy, and an Attempt at a Vindication of Shakespeare . . . ," *Miscellaneous Letters and Essays,* p. 87.

16. "An Essay at a Vindication of Love in Tragedies, against Rapin and Mr. Rymer, directed to Mr. Dennis," *Miscellaneous Letters and Essays,* p. 146.

17. These logically contradictory attitudes persisted long in English critical literature. Wellek calls attention to it in Johnson's *Lives of the English Poets.* "This view of a progress of English poetry toward an ideal scientific norm attained especially by Pope is curiously enough combined in Johnson with a constant recognition of the historical point of view and pleadings for a relativity of standards. He recognizes that 'wit has its changes and fashions and at different times, takes different forms.' He explicitly states that 'to judge rightly of an author, we must transport ourselves to his time, and examine what were the wants of his contemporaries, and what were his means of supplying them.' However, he uses the historical argument largely as an apology for shortcomings and mistakes in older literature" (*The Rise of English Literary History,* p. 139).

# Notes

18. "An Essay at a Vindication of the Love-Verses of Cowley and Waller, etc. . . . Directed to Mr. Congreve," *Miscellaneous Letters and Essays,* pp. 210, 211-212. Jones connects the relativism of this essay with the medical relativism of the physicians of the new science ("Science and Criticism . . ."). It appears though that some simply denied to medicine the progress they accorded to the other sciences. In the preface to his *Iphigenia* (1700), Dennis castigates "our Empiricks in Poetry" who depart from Horace and Aristotle with as little reason as "our Medicinal Quacks" depart from Galen and Hippocrates (Hooker, II, 390). And Dryden illustrates his preference for epic over tragedy by a medical simile which implies the same prejudice ("Dedication of the Aeneis" [1697], Ker, II, 158).

19. "An Essay upon Epick Poetry," *Essays upon Several Subjects,* pp. 9-11, 12, 13.

20. *Essays upon Several Subjects,* pp. 13, 32-33, 100, 160. Blackmore renders a generally favorable verdict on the "Schism of *Perrault*" ("An Appendix" to "An Essay upon Epick Poetry," pp. 158-159). In the critical war in France he can see some right on both sides but thinks the reformers did the greater service "to improve the Art of Poetry" (pp. 159-161).

21. Ferrand Spence, *Miscellanea: or Various Discourses,* "The Preface" [no pag.].

22. "Of Ancient and Modern Tragedy," *The Works of . . . St. Evremond made English . . . by Mr. Des Maizeaux,* II, 12-13.

23. Hooker, I, 208, 210, 213, 407.

24. *An Epistle to a Friend Concerning Poetry* (1700), ll. 260-274, 350-353.

25. *A Discourse on Criticism and the Liberty of Writing* (1707), [p. 9].

26. *A Full Enquiry into the True Nature of Pastoral* (1717), p. 58. Purney declares earlier in his essay that pastoral poets have not tried "to raise the Poem to any greater

Perfection than they found it in . . . ," whereas epic, tragedy, and comedy have been steadily improved (p. 9).

27. *A Full Enquiry,* p. 71.
28. His purpose was to examine "the origin, the antiquity, the growth, the change, and the completement of Satire among the Romans; to describe, if not define, the nature of that poem, with the several sorts of it; to compare the excellencies of Horace, Persius, and Juvenal, and show the particular manners of their satires; and, lastly, to give an account of this new way of version [i.e., translation], which is attempted in our performance" (Ker, II, 42).
29. This has been ably explained by Donald M. Foerster (*Homer in English Criticism,* pp. 8-9).

## NOTES TO CHAPTER 7

1. Ker, II, 86, 87.
2. *A Treatise de Carmine Pastorali Written by Rapin,* p. 67.
3. "The Original . . . of Satire," Ker, II, 25, 96.
4. Cf. "And thus I have given the history of Satire, and derived it as far as from Ennius to your Lordship [Earl of Dorset]; that is, from its first rudiments of barbarity to its last polishing and perfection . . ." (Ker, II, 99). And in reference to Chaucer's allegedly imperfect versification: "We can only say that he lived in the infancy of our poetry, and that nothing is brought to perfection at the first. We must be children before we grow men" ("Preface to the Fables" [1700], II, 259).
5. "Preface to the Fables," Ker, II, 259. ". . . and our numbers were in their nonage till these last [Waller and Denham] appeared."
6. "The Original . . . of Satire," Ker, II, 33-34, 36.

# Notes

7. "Heads of an Answer to Rymer," *Lives of the English Poets by Samuel Johnson*, I, 473.

8. It has this in common with later absolutisms, especially modern ones. Much of the "new criticism" is a rediscovery and reaffirmation of older theory. Most recently, the so-called Chicago school has urged an even more rigid neo-Aristotelianism in literary aesthetics. Though in this movement there is a conscious adaptation of Aristotle's method, its practitioners cannot justly be charged with "neo-Rymerism." "The program of the Chicago school," Hoyt Trowbridge writes, "is not by any means a sterile formalism, an attempt to revive old slogans and rules and to judge a living poetry by outmoded critical dogma. By its nature as an inductive science, poetics must keep pace with poetry, and the true Aristotelian will try to bring Aristotle himself up to date" ("Aristotle and the 'New Criticism,'" *Sewanee Review*, LII [1944], 552).

9. Gildon does this when he defends love themes in tragedy. He analyzes this ingredient as he finds it in Dryden's *All for Love* and Otway's *Venice Preserved* (and in ancient epic) and considers it a proper one for a genre whose function Aristotle had declared to be the purgation of certain passions through their representation ("An Essay at a Vindication of Love in Tragedies," *Miscellaneous Letters and Essays*, pp. 145-171). Thus Gildon's promised rejection of ipse dixit proves ultimately to be no more than an adaptation of it to modern literary practice. In effect, this amounts to discriminating between minor and major rules. Dennis openly advocates this. In "The Grounds of Criticism in Poetry" (1704), he allows for the infraction of minor rules (concerning means) to avoid violation of the major ones. He believes in fact that Milton had surpassed the ancient epic poets by so doing. Of course, violation of the fundamentals was intolerable as subverting the *end* (Hooker, I, 331).

# Notes

10. Such a critical "summing up" or "readjustment of the sights" was, T. S. Eliot thinks, the peculiar service performed for English criticism by Matthew Arnold in his day as it had been earlier by Coleridge and Dryden in theirs. " 'Pure' artistic appreciation is to my thinking only an ideal, when not merely a figment, and must be, so long as the appreciation of art is an affair of limited and transient human beings existing in space and time. Both artist and audience are limited. . . . Hence each new master of criticism performs a useful service merely by the fact that his errors are of a different kind from the last; and the longer the sequence of critics we have, the greater amount of correction is possible" (*The Use of Poetry and the Use of Criticism*, p. 109).

11. *Selected Essays: 1917-1932*, pp. 4-5.

12. This particular essay is, in fact, more in the spirit of the old absolutism than the new. Shakespeare is judged simply "upon the Rules and Writings of the Ancients" (Hooker, II, 17).

13. The popularity of *Paradise Lost* undoubtedly did much to promote this idea. An interesting instance may be found in a book written by Henry Felton in 1709. A classical scholar addressing his noble pupil, Felton holds uncompromisingly to his conviction of the superiority of the classics. "*Milton,* alone in *Epic* Writing hath transcended the *Greek* and the *Latin* Poet: He hath excelled the *First* in the Force and Richness of Imagination; and hath rivalled the *Last* in Justness of Thought, and Exactness of the Work" (*A Dissertation on Reading the Classics, and Forming a Just Style* . . . , pp. 234-235). "*Milton* himself, as Great a genius as he was, oweth his Superiority over *Homer* and *Virgil*, in Majesty of Thought, and Splendor of Expression, to the Scriptures: They are the Fountain from which he derived his Light; the Sacred Treasure that enriched

# Notes

his Fancy, and furnished him with all the Truth and Wonders of God and his Creation . . ." (p. 95).

14. Though he did subscribe to it. He believed that a tragedy, for instance, "ought to be a very Solemn Lecture, inculcating a particular Providence, and shewing it plainly protecting the Good, and chastizing the Bad, or at least the Violent; and that, if it is otherwise, it is either an empty Amusement, or a scandalous and pernicious Libel upon the Government of the World" ("The Advancement . . . of Modern Poetry" [1701], Hooker, I, 200).

15. Hooker, I, 215, 216. Dennis drew a distinction between "ordinary Passion" and "Enthusiasm," the latter characteristic of the very greatest poetry (pp. 215-216).

16. Hooker, I, 215.

17. "The Grounds of Criticism in Poetry," Hooker, I, 331, 332. In this respect the remarks of his biographer are misleading. "In spirit Dennis was really with the moderns, for his scheme for the reformation of poetry was frankly intended to raise them to the level of the ancients. . . . He further maintained that . . . the moderns might attain to the same excellence" (H. G. Paul, *John Dennis*, pp. 151-152).

18. Hooker, I, 361.

19. Much greater, I think, than that implied in the certainly partial and possibly partisan view of Dennis as the humorless attacker of Pope. Authoritative correction of this view is not entirely lacking. "Dennis' *Usefulness of the stage, Advancement and reformation of modern poetry,* and *Grounds of criticism in poetry,*" Austin Warren writes, ". . . deserve high rank in the history of English criticism and retain more than historical interest. . . . His classicism rests on the double pillars of Milton and Dryden, the two seventeenth centuries. In modern comedy his taste is massively sound . . ." (Review of E. N. Hooker's *The Critical Works of John Dennis,* Vol. II, in *PQ,* XXIV [April 1945], 141). For

his religious theory, Warren feels, "he makes a good case," and a parallel motif in modern criticism warns against its hasty dismissal as dated religiosity.

20. Equally misleading is the conclusion that neoclassical critics were either authoritarian or impressionistic. "Most of the writers who rebelled against the rules of the neo-classic school in the eighteenth century had nothing to offer in their stead except mere impressionism. They simply extended Sir William Temple's doctrine of taste which discovers the beauties beyond the rules. . . . But the business of a critic is not only to discern what is beautiful but also to give reasons for the faith that is in him. If he does not do it, then we have anarchy in criticism. But this aspect of criticism was not developed till the time of Coleridge, who was as much opposed to lawlessness in criticism as to the Rules" (D. S. Sarma, "Two Minor Critics of the Age of Pope," *MLR,* XIV [October 1919], 387). Sarma excepted Welsted, but both Dryden and Dennis have prior and better claims.

## NOTES TO CHAPTER 8

1. Curt A. Zimansky, "The Critical Works of Thomas Rymer with *Edgar An Heroic Tragedy,*" pp. xiv-xv.
2. "Upon Critics Who Judge of Modern Plays Precisely by the Rules of the Antients" (1678?), Spingarn, II, 278-281.

# List of Works Cited

Atkins, J. W. H. *English Literary Criticism: 17th and 18th Centuries.* London: Methuen, 1951.

——. *English Literary Criticism: The Renascence.* London: Methuen, 1947.

Bacon, Francis. *The Works,* ed. Basil Montague. 3 vols., Philadelphia: M. Murphy, 1876.

Bate, Walter Jackson. *From Classic to Romantic.* Cambridge: Harvard University Press, 1949.

Blackmore, Sir Richard. *Essays upon Several Subjects.* London, 1716.

Blackwell, Thomas. *An Enquiry into the Life and Writings of Homer.* 2nd. ed., London, 1736.

Blount, Sir Thomas Pope. *De Re Poetica.* London, 1694.

Bosker, A. *Literary Criticism in the Age of Johnson.* Groningen, The Hague: J. B. Wolters, 1930.

Bredvold, Louis I. *The Intellectual Milieu of John Dryden.* Ann Arbor: University of Michigan Press, 1934.

Brooks, Cleanth. "Criticism, History and Critical Relativism," in *The Well Wrought Urn.* New York: Harcourt, Brace, 1947, pp. 197-225.

——. (See Muller, H. J.)

Burlingame, Anne Elizabeth. *The Battle of the Books in Its Historical Setting.* New York: B. W. Huebsch, 1920.

# List of Works Cited

Bury, J. B. *The Idea of Progress. An Inquiry into Its Origin and Growth*. New York: Macmillan, 1932.

Bysshe, Edward. *The Art of English Poetry*. 8th ed., London, 1737.

Cobb, Samuel. *Discourse on Criticism and Of Poetry. The Augustan Reprint Society Publication no. 1*, Series Two (July 1946).

Crane, R. S., ed. *Critics and Criticism Ancient and Modern*. Chicago: University of Chicago Press (Copyright 1952 by the University of Chicago).

Creech, Thomas, trans. *Rapin's De Carmine Pastorali. The Augustan Reprint Society Publication no. 3*, Series Two (July 1947).

Dennis, John. *The Critical Works of John Dennis*, ed. Edward Niles Hooker. 2 vols., Baltimore: Johns Hopkins Press, 1939, 1943.

Dryden, John. *Essays of John Dryden*, ed. W. P. Ker. 2 vols., Oxford: Clarendon Press, 1900.

——. "Heads of an Answer to Rymer," in "Dryden," *Lives of the English Poets by Samuel Johnson, Ll.D.*, ed. G. B. Hill. 3 vols., Oxford: Clarendon Press, 1945, I, 471-479.

Durham, Willard, ed. *Critical Essays of the Eighteenth Century 1700-1725*. New Haven: Yale University Press, 1915.

Eliot, T. S. *The Use of Poetry and the Use of Criticism*. Cambridge: Harvard University Press, 1933.

——. "Tradition and the Individual Talent," in *Selected Essays: 1917-1932*. New York: Harcourt, Brace, 1932.

Felton, Henry. *A Dissertation on Reading the Classics, and Forming a Just Style*. 5th ed., London, 1758.

# List of Works Cited

Foerster, Donald M. *Homer in English Criticism: The Historical Approach in the Eighteenth Century*. New Haven: Yale University Press, 1947.

France, Anatole. *La Vie Littéraire*. Première Série. Paris: Calmann-Lévy, n.d.

Gallaway, Francis. *Reason, Rule, and Revolt in English Classicism*. New York: Scribner, 1940.

Gildon, Charles. *Miscellaneous Letters and Essays, on Several Subjects* . . . London, 1694.

Greene, Theodore Meyer. *The Arts and the Art of Criticism*. Princeton: Princeton University Press, 1940.

Hadley, Frances Willard. "The Theory of Milieu in English Criticism from 1660 to 1801." *Abstracts of Theses. Humanistic Series* . . . , *University of Chicago*, IV (September 1925-June 1926). Chicago: University of Chicago Press, 1928, 321-324.

Hooker, Edward Niles. (See Dennis.)

Hulme, T. E. *Speculations: Essays on Humanism and the Philosophy of Art*, ed. Herbert Read. New York: Harcourt, Brace, 1924.

Jones, Richard Foster. *Ancients and Moderns: A Study of the Background of the Battle of the Books*. Washington University Studies, New Series (Language and Literature), no. 6. St. Louis, 1936.

——. "Science and Criticism in the Neo-Classical Age of English Literature." *JHI*, I (October 1940), 381-412.

Jonson, Ben. "Timber: or, Discoveries," in *Ben Jonson*, ed. C. M. Herford and Evelyn Simpson. 11 vols., Oxford: Clarendon Press, 1925-1952, VIII (1947), 563-649.

Ker, W. P. (See Dryden.)

# List of Works Cited

Locke, John. *An Essay Concerning Human Understanding*, abr. and ed. A. S. Pringle-Pattison. Oxford: Clarendon Press, 1924.

Marburg, Clara. *Sir William Temple: A Seventeenth Century "Libertin."* New Haven: Yale University Press, 1932.

Miller, G. M. *The Historical Point of View in English Literary Criticism from 1570-1770*. Anglistische Forschungen, Vol. XXXV. Heidleberg: Carl Winter, 1913.

Muller, Herbert J. *Science and Criticism*. New Haven: Yale University Press, 1943.

—— and Cleanth Brooks. "The Relative and the Absolute: An Exchange of Views." *Sewanee Review*, LVII (1949), 357-377.

Oldmixon, John. *A Pastoral Poem on the Victories at Schellenburg and Blenheim . . . with a Large Preface, Shewing the Antiquity and Dignity of Pastoral Poetry . . .* London, 1704.

Paul, H. G. *John Dennis: His Life and Criticism*. New York: Columbia University Press, 1911.

Pepper, Stephen C. *The Basis of Criticism in the Arts*. Cambridge: Harvard University Press, 1946.

Pottle, Frederick A. *The Idiom of Poetry*. Ithaca: Cornell University Press, 1946.

Purney, Thomas. *A Full Enquiry into the True Nature of Pastoral. The Augustan Reprint Society Publication no. 4,* Series Two (January 1948).

Rushton, Urban J. P. "The Development of Historical Criticism in England, 1532-1700." Unpublished Princeton University doctoral dissertation, 1940.

# List of Works Cited

Rymer, Thomas. *A Short View of Tragedy*. London, 1693 [1692].

——. *The Tragedies of the Last Age*. 2nd ed., London, 1692.

Saint-Évremond, Seigneur de [Charles de Marguetel de Saint-Denis]. *Miscellanea: or Various Discourses . . . By the Sieur de Saint Evremont . . . made English By Ferrand Spence*. London, 1686.

——. *The Works of Monsieur De St. Evremond made English from the French Original . . . by Mr. Des Maizeaux . . . in Three Volumes*. London, 1714.

Saintsbury, George. *A History of Criticism and Literary Taste in Europe*. 3 vols., New York: Humanities Press, 1950.

——. "Elizabethan Criticism," *CHEL*. New York: Macmillan, 1933, III, 329-355.

Sarma, D. S. "Two Minor Critics of the Age of Pope." *MLR*, XIV (October 1919), 386-390.

Smith, David Nichol. *John Dryden*. Cambridge: The University Press, 1950.

Smith, G. Gregory. *Elizabethan Critical Essays*. 2 vols., London: Oxford University Press, 1904.

Spence, Ferrand. (See Saint-Évremond.)

Spingarn, J. E. *A History of Literary Criticism in the Renaissance*. New York: Columbia University Press, 1920.

——, ed. *Critical Essays of the Seventeenth Century*. 3 vols., Oxford: Clarendon Press, 1908-1909.

Sprague, Arthur Colby, ed. *Samuel Daniel: Poems and a Defence of Ryme*. Cambridge: Harvard University Press, 1930.

Stephen, Sir Leslie. *English Literature and Society in the Eighteenth Century*. London: Duckworth, 1947.

# List of Works Cited

Taeusch, Henry William. "The Influence of the Idea of Progress on English Literary Criticism to 1700." *Harvard University, Graduate School of Arts and Sciences, Summaries of Theses . . . Doctor of Philosophy 1928.* Cambridge: Harvard University Press, 1931, pp. 154-155.

Thorpe, Clarence De Witt. *The Aesthetic Theory of Thomas Hobbes.* Ann Arbor: University of Michigan Press, 1940.

Trowbridge, Hoyt. "Aristotle and the 'New Criticism.'" *Sewanee Review,* LII (1944), 537-555.

——. "The Place of the Rules in Dryden's Criticism." *MP,* XLIV (November 1946), 85-96. (Copyright 1946 by the University of Chicago.)

Warren, Austin. Review of E. N. Hooker's *The Critical Works of John Dennis.* Vol. II. *PQ,* XXIV (April 1945), 140-141.

——. (See Wellek.)

Wellek, René. *The Rise of English Literary History.* Chapel Hill: University of North Carolina Press, 1941.

—— and Austin Warren. *Theory of Literature.* New York: Harcourt, Brace, 1949.

Wesley, Samuel. *Epistle to a Friend Concerning Poetry and the Essay on Heroic Poetry. The Augustan Reprint Society Publication no. 2,* Series Two (January 1947).

Willey, Basil. *The Eighteenth Century Background.* London: Chatto and Windus, 1940.

——. *The Seventeenth Century Background.* London: Chatto and Windus, 1946 [1934].

Wood, Paul Spencer. "The Opposition to Neo-Classicism in England between 1660 and 1700." *PMLA,* XLIII (March 1928), 182-197.

# List of Works Cited

Young, Edward. *Conjectures on Original Composition,* ed. Edith J. Morley. London: Longmans, Green, 1918.

Zimansky, Curt Arno, ed. "The Critical Works of Thomas Rymer with *Edgar An Heroic Tragedy.*" Unpublished Princeton University doctoral dissertation, 1937.

# Index

Absolutism, critical: historical, 3, 4, 23, 115, 116, 121,
127; of end, 21, 35-36 (defined), 35-49, 50, 73, 130,
134n24; of means and end,
21 (defined), 28-35, 73, 129,
130, 141n45; and dogma-
tism, 38, 84, 91, 92, 120,
126, 128, 130

Absolutism, new, 3, 5, 54, 58,
101, 105, 107, 109, 113, 114,
115-126, 154n12

"Ancients" and "Moderns,"
27, 28, 48, 59, 87, 94-96, 98,
102, 110, 114, 122, 141n45,
149n8

Ariosto, Ludovico, 23, 25, 104

Aristotle, 5, 10, 20, 23, 27-33
passim, 38, 47-48, 54, 56-57,
58, 59, 60, 73, 95, 98-107
passim, 111, 119, 122, 124-
125, 151n18, 153n8,n9

Arnold, Matthew, 20, 150n-
13, 154n10

Ascham, Roger, 9, 10, 11, 12,
14, 23

Atkins, J. W. H., 24, 134n26,
143n25, 148n5

Bacon, Francis, 27, 94, 98,
109

Bate, W. J., 137n9, 149n8

Beaumont, Francis, 81

Bentley, Richard, 84

Blackmore, Sir Richard, 57,
76-77, 103-105, 107, 135n3,
136n6, 145n13, 147n33, 151-
n20

Blackwell, Thomas, 68-69,
85-86

Blount, Sir Thomas Pope, 97

Boccaccio, Giovanni, 115

Boileau, Nicolas, 75, 77,
144n9

Bosker, A., 143n26, 146n28,
149n8

Bredvold, Louis I., 133n15,
143n23

Bridges, Robert, 146n20

Brontë, Emily, 51

Brooks, Cleanth, 138n24

Burlingame, Anne Elizabeth,
148n5

Bury, J. B., 92, 147n2, 148n3,
149n9

Butler, Samuel (1612-1680),
129

Bysshe, Edward, 65

# Index

Campion, Thomas, 16, 17, 19

Catullus, 103

Chapman, George, 38, 39

Chaucer, Geoffrey, 16, 65, 115, 118, 152n4

Cicero, 97, 132n5

Climate, 16, 43, 55, 70, 71, 86, 103, 144n2, 146n22

Cobb, Samuel, 111

Colbatch, Sir John, 110

Coleridge, S. T., 20, 150n13, 154n10, 156n20

Collier, Jeremy, 136n6

Comedy, 60, 63, 68, 72, 136n-6, 143n16. *See also* Genre

Congreve, William, 143n16

Corneille, Pierre, 106

Cowley, Abraham, 39, 71, 75, 80, 83, 103, 145n18

Creech, Thomas, 116

Cycles theory of culture, 95, 142n10, 148n6

Dacier, André, 58

Daniel, Samuel, 9, 14, 17-22, 23, 25, 28, 134n22

Davenant, Sir William, 37, 45, 74, 98-99

Decorum, 24, 105

Definition in aesthetics, 117, 119, 123, 138n24

Demosthenes, 97, 132n5

Denham, Sir John, 39, 118, 152n4

Dennis, John, 4, 26, 31, 47, 55-58, 59, 68, 73-74, 77-79, 82-83, 86-91 *passim,* 101, 107-109, 121-126, 129, 131, 140n44, 142n9, 143n16, 145-n15, 151n18, 153n9, 155n-15,n17,n19, 156n20

Descartes, René, 27, 95, 101, 106

Donne, John, 47

Dryden, John, 4, 5, 26, 34, 37-48 *passim,* 53, 54, 55, 63, 64, 72, 75-76, 79, 80-81, 82, 83, 84, 87, 109, 111, 113, 115-119, 121, 124, 125, 130, 135n2, 138n22, 139n33, 140n43,n44, 145n9, 146n-24, 151n18, 153n9, 154n10, 155n19, 156n20

Eddington, Sir Arthur, 136n8

Einstein, Albert, 136n8

E. K., 22

Eliot, T. S., 120-121, 150n13, 154n10

"Empiricks" in poetic theory, 30, 151n18

Ennius, 10, 117, 118, 152n4

Environmentalism, 71, 84, 89, 90, 91, 100, 102, 105, 108, 109, 111

Epic, 23-24, 34, 36, 37, 45, 57, 67, 74-79, 85, 86, 87, 88-89, 90, 99, 104, 118-119, 122, 123, 124, 133n5, 139n33, 140n41, 145n13,n15, 147-n33, 153n9, 154n13. *See also* Genre

Epicurus, 95

Etherege, Sir George, 68

Euripides, 55
Evaluation, 4, 6, 14, 21, 25, 49, 50-52, 58, 64, 71, 72, 79, 81, 83, 130, 138n24

Faraday, Michael, 150n13
Farquhar, George, 60-61
Felton, Henry, 154n13
Flecknoe, Richard, 58
Fletcher, John, 43, 44, 61
Foerster, Donald M., 131n3, 152n29
Fontenelle, Bernard de, 94, 95, 149n8
"Foundation" and "Super-structures," 44-45, 48
France, Anatole, 141n3
Freedom, political, 89, 143n-16

Galen, 110, 151n18
Gallaway, Francis, 141n46, 145n18, 148n5
Gascoigne, George, 22
Gassendi, Pierre, 106
Genre, 6, 21, 37, 45, 59, 66, 73, 74, 79, 90, 112, 113, 117, 132n5, 138n24, 147n33, 153-n9; decay of, 79, 86-90
Gildon, Charles, 26, 32, 33, 34, 48, 58-60, 65, 84, 101-103, 141n45, 145n11, 153n9
Greene, Theodore Meyer, 132n3

Hadley, Frances Willard, 144n2

Hardy, Thomas, 21
Harington, Sir John, 23-24, 25
Harvey, Gabriel, 11, 12
Harvey, William, 95
Heliodorus, 105
Herbert of Cherbury, 29
Hippocrates, 103, 151n18
Historical criticism, 6, 13, 23, 24, 32, 49, 66, 90, 116, 119-120, 150n17; and relativism, 3-7, 14, 19, 20, 84, 115, 126, 127, 131n3, 132n5
Hobbes, Thomas, 7, 37, 63, 74, 95
Homer, 16, 23, 26, 34, 38, 45, 46, 47, 57, 58, 62, 65, 67, 68, 77, 85-88 *passim*, 98, 99, 111, 113, 117, 119, 132n5, 140n43, 145n15, 154n13
Hooker, Edward Niles, 141n44
Horace, 10, 13, 27, 39, 43, 46, 47, 56, 111, 116, 117, 118, 136n6, 151n18, 152n28
Howard, Sir Robert, 42, 45, 62
Hughes, John, 66-67
Hulme, T. E., 146n20
Humanism, 9, 10, 11
"Humours," 60, 61, 72, 143n16

Idiom, "exhaustion" of, 80-81, 145n20
Imitation, 10, 13, 19, 27, 30,

34, 35, 38, 39, 44, 74, 98-99, 132n5

Impressionism, 7, 18, 23, 24, 52, 129, 156n20

Ipse dixit, 10, 101, 104, 153n9

James I, King, 22

Johnson, Samuel, 150n17

Jones, R. F., 93, 134n1, 135-n2, 147n2, 148n5, 151n18

Jonson, Ben, 31, 36, 41, 42, 61, 81, 82, 98-99, 120

Juvenal, 46, 116, 117, 152n28

Keats, John, 80

Ker, W. P., 135n2

Langbaine, Gerard, 81

Language, 11-19 *passim*, 36-41, 44, 65, 70, 74, 76, 82, 86, 87, 88-89, 91, 92, 139n33

Le Bossu, René, 58, 85

Literary "climate," 42-43, 70, 79-84, 91

Literary history, 3, 6, 46, 81, 97, 113, 132n5

Locke, John, 29

Longinus, 38, 73, 89, 119, 124-125

Love theme in tragedy, 55, 59, 101, 153n9

Lucilius, 117

Lucretius, 88

Machinery, epic, 76-79, 90, 118, 145n15

Marburg, Clara, 148n6

Martial, 38

Mathematics, influence of, 27-32, 63, 96, 101, 128, 137-n9

Maxwell, James Clerk, 150n13

Method, 22, 27, 28, 32, 34, 43, 47-48, 55, 57, 62, 81, 85-86, 99, 104, 110, 117, 128, 135-n3, 140n44, 153n8. *See also* Absolutism, critical; Mathematics, influence of; Relativism, critical

Milton, John, 45, 62, 78, 83, 113, 119, 124, 146n22, 148-n2, 153n9, 154n13, 155n19

Muller, Herbert J., 50, 138n24

Nash, Thomas, 16, 22, 133n15

Nature's decay, theory of, 87, 93-94, 110, 147n2, 148n3

Neo-Aristotelians of Chicago, 153n8

"New Criticism," 153n8

Newton, Sir Isaac, 110, 150n13

Norris, John, 97, 149n10

Novel, 21, 51, 90. *See also* Genre

Oldmixon, John, 66, 146n22

Otway, Thomas, 153n9

Ovid, 71, 103, 115

Pascal, Blaise, 149n8

Pastoral, 61-62, 66, 83, 112,

# Index

116-117, 151n26. *See also* Genre
Pater, Walter, 141n3
Paul, H. G., 155n17
Peacham, Henry, 93
Pepper, Stephen C., 51-52, 138n24
Perrault, Charles, 96, 97, 151n20
Persius, 46, 152n28
Phillips, Edward, 36-37
Pindar, 74, 87, 111
Plato, 95
Plautus, 26
Pliny (the younger), 97
Pope, Alexander, 51, 80, 108, 145n15, 150n17, 155n19
Pottle, Frederick, 6, 50, 136n8, 149n13
Pragmatism in literary theory, 36, 43, 61, 77, 129
Progress: of literature, 3, 4, 20, 42, 87, 94, 96-100, 104, 106-114, 115, 117-119, 122, 124, 140n43, 149n9, 150n-17, 151n26; idea of, 4, 70, 92-114, 126, 128, 149n8,-n10; of criticism, 46, 100-102, 104-107, 109, 113, 114, 120, 128, 149n13
Prosody, 11-24 *passim,* 37, 40, 41, 65, 88, 118. *See also* Rhyme
Purgation, tragic, 5, 36, 53, 54, 59, 153n9
Purney, Thomas, 61, 112-113, 151n26

Puttenham, George, 8, 13-16, 19, 20, 24, 25, 133n11,n12

Race, 49, 59, 60, 70, 71-74, 86, 87, 91, 92, 144n2
Rapin, René, 58, 59, 65, 116-117
Relativism, critical: of means (absolutism of end), 22, 36, 41, 43, 47-49, 53, 59, 134n-24, 141n45; of ends, 44, 50-69, 73
Relativism, historical, 3, 18, 19, 23, 55, 59, 66-67, 68, 85, 101, 102, 107, 109, 121, 142n10
Relativism, subjective. *See* Impressionism; Taste
Religion, 24, 29, 36, 44, 45-46, 55, 57, 58, 70, 82, 83, 86, 91, 92, 99, 105, 107, 108, 118, 145n11, 147n33; and modern epic, 45, 74-79, 154n13; in Dennis' poetic theory, 77-78, 121-126, 156n-19
Reynolds, Henry, 30, 93
Rhyme, 9, 11, 12, 14, 15, 17, 19, 20, 22, 25, 37, 80-81, 146n22
Rhyme-blank verse controversy, 11-20, 23, 24
Roscommon, Earl of, 139n30
Royal Society, 28, 75
Rules, critical, 4, 9, 14, 16, 18, 19, 23, 24, 27, 41, 51, 54-62 *passim,* 67, 72, 73, 103-106

169

*passim,* 111, 116, 119, 121, 122, 135n3, 156n20; means and end view of, 28-35, 45-48, 137n22, 153n9

Rymer, Thomas, 5, 21, 29, 30, 31, 32, 43, 45, 47, 52-53, 55, 58, 59, 69, 83, 84, 120, 127, 129-130, 140n44, 153n8

Saint-Évremond, Charles de, 54-55, 72, 105, 106-107, 108, 109, 114, 142n9

Saintsbury, George, 11, 53, 133n16, 134n27

Sarma, D. S., 156n20

Satire, 46-47, 87, 113, 116, 152n28, 152n4. *See also* Genre

Science, influence of, 3, 6, 26-29 *passim,* 32, 96, 98, 100-104, 106-110, 113-114, 118-119, 120, 122, 126, 128, 134n1, 136n8, 149n8,n9, 150n13, 151n18

Seneca, 97

Shakespeare, William, 4, 43, 44, 56, 58, 61, 65, 66, 81, 84, 121, 129, 154n10

Shelley, Percy B., 83

Sidney, Sir Philip, 9, 22, 38, 136n6

Skepticism, 18, 19, 21, 47, 63-64, 133n15, 135n2

Smith, David Nichol, 145n20

Smith, G. Gregory, 9

Soame[s], Sir William, 145n9

Sophocles, 4, 26, 55, 82-83, 86

Spence, Ferrand, 151n21

Spenser, Edmund, 16, 22, 65, 66-67, 84, 104, 118

Spingarn, J. E., 28, 133n6, 149n8

Sprague, A. C., 134n22

Sprat, Bishop Thomas, 75

Stanyhurst, Richard, 11

Steele, Sir Richard, 67

Stephen, Sir Leslie, 86

Sternhold, Thomas, 58

Sublimity, 78, 122-123, 125

Taeusch, H. W., 149n8

Taine, Hippolyte, 74

Tasso, Torquato, 111

Taste, 7, 24, 37, 38, 43, 46, 47, 51, 57, 59-60, 62-65, 66, 70, 84, 105, 129, 132n5, 143n25, 146n22, 147n33, 149n9, 156n20

Temple, Sir William, 32, 64, 76, 79, 88, 95, 143n16, 148n6,n7, 156n20

Theocritus, 62, 112, 116

Thorpe, Clarence De Witt, 63

Tragedy, 4, 5, 31, 36, 41, 43, 44, 47-48, 53, 55-56, 59, 72, 80-81, 82, 87, 101, 113, 119, 122-125 *passim,* 136n6, 145-n13, 155n14. *See also* Genre

Translation, 11, 38-40, 77, 139n30,n31

Trowbridge, Hoyt, 137n22, 153n8

# Index

Versification, 10, 15, 16, 22, 23, 152n4. *See also* Prosody

Virgil, 10, 11, 12, 16, 23, 24, 26, 34, 40, 41, 45, 46, 47, 57, 62, 65, 66, 67, 77, 87, 88, 99, 111, 116-117, 118, 132n5, 154n13

Waller, Edmund, 74, 103, 118, 152n4

Warren, Austin, 142n10, 155n19

Webbe, William, 12-13

Wellek, René, 79, 132n5, 142n10, 150n17

Welsted, Leonard, 27, 32, 148n7, 156n20

Wesley, Samuel, 85, 110

Wilde, Oscar, 141n3

Willey, Basil, 137n9, 140n41

Wood, Paul Spencer, 142n4

Woolf, Virginia, 21

Wordsworth, William, 80

Wotton, William, 88-89, 96, 118, 149n8,n9

Young, Edward, 38

Zimansky, Curt A., 156n1